GW00891394

BOOKS BY ANNE GRAHAM LOTZ

*Jesus in Me: Experiencing the Holy Spirit
as a Constant Companion*

*The Vision of His Glory: Finding Hope
Through the Revelation of Jesus Christ*

God's Story

Just Give Me Jesus

Pursuing MORE of Jesus

Heaven: My Father's House

Why? Trusting God When You Don't Understand

The Magnificent Obsession: Embracing the God-Filled Life

Expecting to See Jesus: A Wake-Up Call for God's People

*Wounded by God's People: Discovering How God's Love
Heals Our Hearts*

*The Daniel Prayer: Prayer That Moves Heaven
and Changes Nations*

The Daniel Key: 20 Choices That Make All the Difference

The Joy of My Heart: Meditating Daily on God's Word

Fixing My Eyes on Jesus: Daily Moments in His Word

Into the Word

Daily Light

*Storming the Gates of Heaven: Prayer That Claims
the Promises of God*

CHILDREN'S BOOK

Heaven: God's Promise for Me

THE LIGHT OF HIS PRESENCE

THE LIGHT of HIS PRESENCE

PRAYERS TO DRAW YOU NEAR
TO THE HEART OF GOD

ANNE GRAHAM LOTZ

Authentic

Copyright © 2020 by Anne Graham Lotz

26 25 24 23 22 21 20   7 6 5 4 3 2 1

Published in 2020 by Authentic Media Limited
PO Box 6326, Bletchley, Milton Keynes MK1 9GG.
www.authenticmedia.co.uk

Published in the United States by Multnomah, an imprint of Random House, a
division of Penguin Random House LLC. Multnomah® and its mountain
colophon are registered trademarks of Penguin Random House LLC.

All rights reserved.
No part of this publication may be reproduced, stored in a retrieval system, or
transmitted in any form or by any means, electronic, mechanical, photocopying,
recording or otherwise, without the prior permission of the publisher or a
licence permitted restricted copying. In the UK such licences are issued by the
Copyright Licensing Angency, 5th Floor, Shakleton House, 4 Battle Bridge
Land, London SE1 2HX.

British Library Cataloguing in Publication Data
A catalogue record for this book is available from the British Library.

ISBN: 978-1-78893-204-2
978-1-78893-207-3 (e-book)

All Scripture quotations, unless otherwise indicated, are taken from the Holy
Bible, New International Version®, NIV®. Copyright © 1973,
1978 by Biblica Inc.™ Used by permission of Zondervan. All rights reserved
worldwide, www.zondervan.com. The "NIV" and "New International Version"
are trademarks registered in the United States
Patent and Trademark Office by Biblica, Inc.™ Scripture quotations
marked (nkjv) are taken from the New King James Version®.
Copyright © 1982 by Thomas Nelson Inc. Used by permission.

Author is represented by Alive Literary Agency, 7680 Goddard Street, Suite
200, Colorado Springs, Colorado 80920, www.aliveliterary.com.

Appendix B is adapted from *The Daniel Prayer* by Anne Graham Lotz.
Copyright © 2016 by Anne Graham Lotz. Used by permission of Zondervan.
www.zondervan.com.

Book design by Susan Turner

Printed and bound by CPI Group (UK) Ltd, Croydon, CR0 4YY

Dedicated to those who struggle in prayer
yet who long to draw near
to the heart of God

One thing I ask of the LORD,
this is what I seek:
that I may dwell in the house of the LORD
all the days of my life,
to gaze upon the beauty of the LORD
and to seek him.
Psalm 27:4

Contents

Introduction

PRAYER HAS BEEN ONE OF THE GREATEST CHALLENGES OF my Christian life. While I know I'm commanded to pray, encouraged to pray, invited to pray, and often compelled to pray, I have still struggled with prayer. My struggle has centered primarily on three areas.

First, I have struggled with concentration—why is it that as soon as I bow my head to pray, my thoughts start to scatter? Instead of truly communicating with God, I think about what I need to fix for supper or what I'm going to wear to a special event or when I can schedule coffee with a friend. Or I'm so tired that I simply doze in the quietness of the hour.

The second area I have struggled with is consistency—making time daily to meet with the Lord in prayer. How often I have been distracted by my chirping phone or interrupted by my dog needing to go out or so busy I jump out of bed at the last minute and into my day without any real prayer at all.

And I have struggled with content—just knowing what to say and how to say it.

As I have sought victory in these three areas, I have asked God to give me solutions. And He has! Setting my alarm for an earlier time—allowing me to meet with the Lord before I begin my day—has helped with consistency. And writing down my prayers has helped not only with content but also with concentration.

In this volume you'll find some of the prayers I have written. These prayers do not cover every crisis or cry, desire or delight, longing or lack, struggle or success, or a myriad of other issues I have taken to the Lord in prayer over the years. But I hope you'll find these prayers a helpful resource to refresh your own conversations with God. Especially if you, too, have struggled with prayer.

While I can't help you set your alarm, I wonder whether reading some of the prayers I have written will help you with your own concentration and content in prayer. As you read them, you may want to make note of the four elements I try to include in my prayers: *worship, confession, thanksgiving,* and *intercession.*

I have made a habit of beginning my prayers by worshipping God for who He is, because as I focus on Him, it's amazing how my own needs and problems are reduced in size compared with who He is. Then I look at myself and confess the sin that now seems obvious, revealed by the light of His holiness and glory. God has used a list of sins to effectively guide me deeper into confession. I have included this list as a resource for you in Appendix B. I do not beat myself up over my sin, but instead, once I have named it for what it is, I move into thanksgiving to the One who has forgiven and cleansed me. At this point, I am ready to present my requests and intercede for others. While not every prayer includes each of these four elements, you will recognize the pattern. I have left some of the pages in this volume blank so you can write down your own prayers, using this pattern if it's helpful.

And remember, the purpose of prayer is not just to get answers. The purpose is to develop an intimate, personal relationship with the One who loves you, gave Himself for you, and longs for you to live in the light of His presence.

My prayer for you as you read this volume is that God will use my struggle with prayer to help you overcome yours. And that, as a result, you will be drawn nearer to the heart of God.

The apostle Paul prayed for the Ephesian followers of Jesus, and I have prayed these words for you:

For this reason
I kneel before the Father,
from whom his whole family in heaven and
on earth derives its name.
I pray that out of his glorious riches
he may strengthen you with power through his Spirit in
your inner being,

so that Christ may dwell in your hearts through faith.
And I pray that you,
being rooted and established in love,
may have power,
together with all the saints,
to grasp how wide and long and high and deep is
the love of Christ,
and to know this love that surpasses knowledge—
that you may be filled to the measure of all the
fullness of God.
Ephesians 3:14–19

THE LIGHT OF HIS PRESENCE

When God puts a burden upon you
He puts His own arm underneath.

—L. B. Cowman

A Prayer of the Weary

Great, Perfect High Priest,

I worship You, the One who understands the feeling of my infirmities.[1] You are tender. Gentle. A bruised reed You will not break. Smoking flax You will not quench.[2] You never grow tired or weary.[3]

I confess that sometimes I do feel weary. Breakable. Lonely as I stand for You and speak out for You when so few others do. You don't blame me for my weariness and weakness. Instead, You sympathize with me. Yet I remember that You have said You set the lonely in families.[4] So I thank You for Your family, for my Christian brothers and sisters who stand beside me shoulder to shoulder and heart to heart, as together we continue to live for You in this increasingly dark, dangerous, and hostile world.

Dear Father God, I ask that You would use me to encourage others—and bring into my life those who will do the same for me. Let us build one another up. Strengthen one another. So that when the Enemy comes in like a flood, assaulting us from every side, on every level and from every angle, we still stand. With spirits battered, maybe. With hearts wounded, maybe. But with sword raised in victory![5] May we continue standing firm!

For the glory of Your great name—*Jesus,*
Amen.

Men ask for a rainbow in the cloud;
but I would ask *more* from Thee.
I would be, in my cloud, myself a
    rainbow—
a minister to others' joy.

—George Matheson

A Prayer for Stormy Days

Awesome, Omnipotent Creator God,
 I worship You, the One . . .
who "laid the earth's foundations,"
who "marked off its dimensions,"
who "shut up the sea behind doors when it burst
 forth from the womb,"
who "made the clouds its garment,"
who "fixed limits for it," and
who said, "This far you may come and no farther;
 here is where your proud waves halt."[1]
I think of when Your disciples struggled in the storm
on Galilee, then called out to You, and You commanded
the wind and waves to be still. And they obeyed![2]

As the storms of life assail me, as those I love face
waves that threaten to submerge them in despair, I ask You
to look on us with mercy. I cry out to You, knowing that
just as the wind and waves know Your voice and respond,

so too are all the forces of this world subject to Your power. I ask that You would speak into our lives the words *Peace! Be still!* Please. For the glory of Your great name.

I ask that You would keep Your promise: "When you pass through the waters, I will be with you; and when you pass through the rivers, they will not sweep over you."[3]

You are Immanuel. God with us. Facing every storm that comes my way, I cling to You in trust.

In the name of the One whom the waves and wind still obey—*Jesus,*

Amen.

Personal Prayer

A true prayer

is

an inventory of needs,

a catalog of necessities,

an exposure of secret wounds,

a revelation of hidden poverty.

—C. H. Spurgeon

A Prayer in the Hardest Times

MAN OF SORROWS,
As I watch the devastation and heartache in the lives of those around me, my spirit cries out, "No. No! *No!*" How can this be? How can You look on and allow such suffering? *Why?*

I will stand at my watch and look to see how You will answer me.[1] In the silence, I seem to hear Your soft whisper echoing what You have said to me before when unexpected and unexplained crises have erupted. Your answer seems to be the same: *Trust Me when you don't understand.*

O God, You have been our Help in ages past. You are our Hope for years to come. And You alone are our Shelter from this stormy blast.[2] You alone are our Refuge and our Strength. You are the Good Shepherd, who will lead us safely through this valley of shadow.[3]

As I reflect on the One whom I am asked to trust, my

soul finds rest. You are my great High Priest, who understands. You are well acquainted with grief. Suffering.[4]

So please, look on all those I love who are in pain, in fear for their future. *Please.* Draw near to them. As they become more focused on the reality of their stark situations, I ask You to balance their feelings of devastation and loss with the comfort of Your presence. Your peace. Your love. Wipe the tears from our eyes. Turn our faces to Yours. Cause us to choose to look up. To look to You. With trust.

I pray this in the name of the One who has given His word, "Never will I leave you; never will I forsake you."[5] *Jesus.*

Amen.

The best disposition for praying
is
that of being
desolate,
forsaken,
stripped of everything.

—Augustine

A Prayer of Surrender

FAIREST LORD JESUS, RULER OF ALL NATURE, LORD of the nations,[1]

I humbly bow before You and give You honor, praise, and glory for the countless blessings You continuously pour out on me. You demonstrate Your compassion through the ordinary people You use to bless me each day. And I glimpse Your love through circumstances that reveal You are gracious, abounding in loving-kindness and truth.[2]

I confess that all too often I overlook Your good and perfect gifts. Instead of rejoicing in Your strength made glorious in my weakness,[3] I am tempted to pride myself on being self-sufficient. I do not glorify You, my God, nor give thanks to You but live as though I have no accountability to You. God of mercy, I confess my desperate need of You. I grieve for the times I have walked away in pride, behaving as if I am in charge of my own life.

You have said in Your Word that if we don't just confess sin with our mouths but truly turn away from it and return to You, You will return to us.[4] In this moment I return to You—I run to You!—and beg You to return to me. I ask You to stir within me a desire for what is true and good. Take from me any tendency toward self-reliance. You have said in Your Word that You are our Rock. Our Shield. Our Stronghold. Our Refuge.[5] When I am tempted to lean on my own strength, teach me instead to hide in You.

In the strong name of Jesus,

Amen.

Personal Prayer

The LORD bless you
and keep you;
the LORD make his face shine upon
    you
and be gracious to you;
the LORD turn his face toward you
and give you peace.

—Numbers 6:24–26

A Prayer for Peace and Protection

G OD OF ABRAHAM, ISAAC, AND JACOB,
You are the eternal I AM. The One who is
age to age the same. There is no shadow of turning with
You. You are fully present in every generation—past,
present, and future. You are the Almighty. Your power
has not been depleted over the millennia of human history. We know that You so loved the world that You gave
us Heaven's treasure when You sent Your only Son over
two thousand years ago to be born as a baby, wrapped in
swaddling clothes, and laid in a manger. Thank You for
the gospel, which tells us that everyone who places faith
in the Baby—who grew, lived, then died as our Savior . . . who now sits on Heaven's throne . . . who is soon
to return and rule the world—will not perish but have
everlasting life.[1] Heaven's miracle available to little dust
people!

Yet I see around me a world that is increasingly desperate! Evil seems to be unrestrained. Babies are aborted, and pieces of their bodies sold. Sex trafficking is thriving. Nations are unraveling. Wars are raging, and it seems that daily I hear rumors of more wars breaking out. I cannot help but feel a sense of turmoil and agitation that surely is a reflection of the war being waged in the invisible realm.

I humbly turn to You now. You alone are the One who makes us dwell in safety. You alone are the One who makes us secure. You alone are God. I turn to You, deeply aware that, in myself, I am unworthy to address You yet confident of access into Your most holy presence through the blood of Your Son and my Savior, the Lord Jesus Christ.

I ask that the fear of the one true, living God would fall on me, my household, my church, my community, my country.

I ask for supernatural wisdom that I and those I love, especially those I serve alongside, would make decisions in line with Your perfect will.

I ask especially that You would draw the leaders in my church, my community, and this country to Yourself. Cause them to put their trust in You so they experience peace both without and within.

I ask that You bless our beloved nation. Protect us. Defend us. Heal us. Unite us. Please continue to use us as a force for good in the world. Keep us steadfast in our commitment to be a friend to Your people.

You are a great prayer-hearing, prayer-answering, covenant-keeping, miracle-working God. Hear my prayer and bless this nation with the peace that only the power of the gospel can bring to our hearts and lives.

For the glory of Your great name—*Jesus,*
Amen.

There is no way
of learning faith
except by trial.
It is God's school of faith,
and it is far better for us to learn to
     trust God
than to enjoy life.

—A. B. Simpson

A Prayer for Unshakable Trust

O GOD OF CREATION,
I bow before You, acknowledging Your greatness and Your glory. No one compares to You. No one is Your equal. I look at Your creation and marvel at the infinite power and wisdom that are Yours. Nothing is beyond Your reach. You are the One who "brings out the starry host one by one and calls them each by name. Because of [Your] great power and mighty strength, not one of them is missing." You are the One who "has pitched a tent for the sun. . . . It rises at one end of the heavens and makes its circuit to the other; nothing is hidden from its heat." "Where can I go from your Spirit? Where can I flee from your presence? If I go up to the heavens, you are there; if I make my bed in the depths, you are there."[1] There is nowhere in all the universe where You are not.

Surely Your arm "is not too short to save, nor [Your] ear too dull to hear."[2]

Yet I confess that as I look around at the mess our world is in—when terrorists strike; when floods, fires, tornadoes, and storms ravage our land; when national leaders don't lead; when business leaders lie; when political leaders put their own interests before the people's; when spiritual leaders contradict Your Word—I find myself asking, *What's going on? Where are You?*

The Enemy whispers lies, tempting me to think You are . . .

distracted, disengaged, distant,
inattentive, inactive, impotent,
outmaneuvered, outmoded, outclassed,
unable, unaffected, and even unaware
of our fear, our helplessness, our confusion, our
    outrage.

Why do You seem so small while our problems, disasters, and enemies seem so large?

So I ask, almighty God, that You would strengthen my resolve to place my trust in You. Give me the courage to declare that even if "the kings of the earth take their stand and the rulers gather together against the LORD,"[3] I will trust in You. If "the earth give[s] way and the mountains fall into the heart of the sea, though its waters roar and foam and the mountains quake with their surging,"[4] I will trust in You.

Though "nations are in uproar, kingdoms fall,"[5] I will trust in You. When "the wicked draw the sword and bend the bow to bring down the poor and needy, to slay those whose ways are upright,"[6] I will trust in You.

I trust You!

In the powerful, unshakable, unstoppable name of Jesus, Amen.

Do not pray for easy lives;
pray to be stronger men!
Do not pray for tasks equal to your
powers;
pray for powers equal to your tasks!
Then the doing of your work will be no
miracle.
But you shall be a miracle.

—Phillips Brooks

A Prayer to Be a Light in the Darkness

Light of the World,
Who is like You, "majestic in holiness, awesome in glory, working wonders"?[1] I long for the day when my faith becomes sight and the whole world is filled with the glory of who You are. My highest joy will be to see You face to face, to gather around Your throne with multitudes from every tribe, language, people, and nation that You have purchased with the blood of Your own Son . . . and worship You.[2]

Most holy God, even as I anticipate that glorious day, I feel compelled to confess my sin. You are righteous. I am not. You always do the right thing. I have done wrong. How often I have enjoyed the riches of Your blessings yet have failed to thank You. My silence when receiving accolades gives the false impression that the credit is due me instead of You. At times I have been intimidated when others have contradicted Your Word and therefore have not refuted their false claims. Have I treated life casually by abusing my health? Have I passed by the needy uncaringly, feeling they are not my responsibility? Have I defiantly made demands of You, instead of gratefully accepting what You give me? I am so sorry.

Today I turn around. I return to You. I run to You. I cling to You. I plead with You.

Fountainhead of all blessing, bless me. Not because I deserve it, but because I ask in Jesus's name. Make me into a vessel of honor, "an instrument for noble purposes, made holy, useful to the Master and prepared to do any good work."[3] I know the night is coming when work for You will cease. Help me redeem the time. Use me now for Your kingdom and Your glory. Open my lips to boldly and fearlessly make known the gospel: the good news of redemption for the past . . . hope for the future . . . joy for the present regardless of circumstances . . . love that is unconditional, boundless, and eternal . . . found at the cross. Open my lips to give Jesus to a world that is increasingly desperate. Use me as an ambassador of peace on earth by leading people into a right relationship first with You, then with one another. When the world around me unravels, help me stand strong on my faith in You. And when people see me standing strong, help them see You.

Use me to turn on the light.

For the glory of Your great name—*Jesus,*
Amen.

Personal Prayer

Since we have been justified through
    faith,
we have peace with God
through our Lord Jesus Christ,
through whom we have gained access by
    faith into this grace in which we now
    stand.
And we rejoice in the hope of the glory of
    God.

—Romans 5:1–2

A Prayer for God's Grace and Glory

G REAT COVENANT-KEEPING GOD,
     I know that no one and nothing is hidden from You in this life or in the next. In this generation, in the last generation, or in the next generation. In the visible world or in the invisible world. You are omniscient. No one and nothing is lost to You. No one can go where You are not. We cannot escape You in the highest heaven or in the lowest hell.[1] You are omnipresent. One day every voice raised in profanity, obscenity, and blasphemy will have to acknowledge that You are King of kings and Lord of lords. You are omnipotent. One day Your glory will fill the earth as the waters cover the sea.[2] You are enduringly strong. You are entirely sincere. You are eternally steadfast. You are unfailingly gracious.

    I depend on Your grace as I confess . . .

    my ingratitude, recognizing how often I neglect to
        thank You for an answered prayer or a blessing.

my neglect of Your Word.

my doubt that You will do as You have promised.

my lackluster prayers, which at times are little more than spiritual chattering, daydreaming and fantasizing instead of fervent conversation with You.

my lack of concern for the lost, evidenced by my timidity in witnessing.

my inadequacy that I use as an excuse for disobedience.

my hypocrisy as I let others think I'm more spiritual than I am.

my prideful tendency toward self-deception as I am impressed by my own reputation.

God of grace, cleanse me of my sin. All of it. Then fill my life with Your Spirit and my home with Your glory. Ignite the fire of revival in my heart. Protect me. Defend me. Comfort me. Empower me. Equip me as I put on the full armor of God so I can stand against the devil's schemes as I watch expectantly for Your return.[3] Even so, come quickly, Lord Jesus![4]

For the glory of Your great name—*Jesus,*
Amen.

Turn the Bible into prayer.

—Robert Murray McCheyne

O Lord,
the great and awesome God,
who keeps his covenant of love
with all who love him
and obey his commands,
we have sinned and done wrong.
We have been wicked and have rebelled;
we have turned away from your
    commands and laws. . . .
Now, O Lord our God,
who brought your people out of Egypt
with a mighty hand
and who made for yourself a name
that endures to this day,
we have sinned,
we have done wrong.

O Lord,
in keeping with all your righteous acts,
turn away your anger and your wrath. . . .
Now, our God,
hear the prayers and petitions of your
     servant.
For your sake, O Lord. . . .
Give ear, O God, and hear;
open your eyes and see. . . .
We do not make requests of you because
     we are righteous,
but because of your great mercy.
O Lord, listen!
O Lord, forgive!
O Lord, hear and act!
For your sake, O my God, do not delay,
because . . . your people bear your Name.

—Daniel 9:4–5, 15–19

Personal Prayer

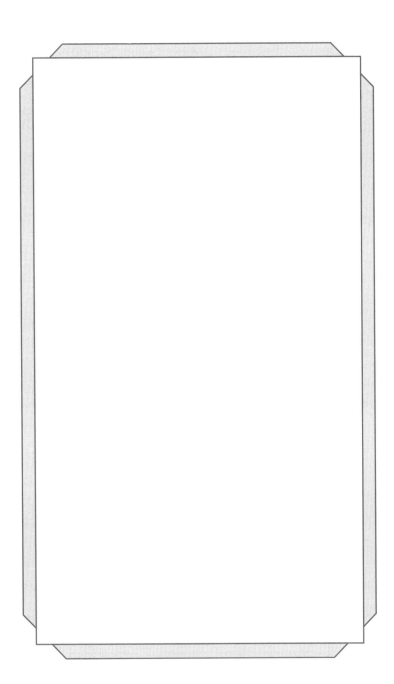

This is the assurance we have
in approaching God:
that if we ask anything according to
    his will,
he hears us.
And if we know that he hears us—
whatever we ask—
we know that we have what we
    asked of him.

                              —1 John 5:14–15

A Prayer to Trust in God's Provision

Great Creator God,
I worship You, the Father's only begotten Son, the One to whom the Father has given everything. You are His Heir to all things. You hold the world in the palm of Your hand, yet You are the same One who sees when a sparrow falls. The same One who clothes the lilies of the field. The same One who fed five thousand hungry men and their families with five loaves and two fish.[1] You have promised to meet all my needs according to the riches of Your glory, because You are Jehovah Jireh, the Lord our Provider.[2]

> I repent of hoarding my own wealth when You have freely given me all things.
> I repent of closing my eyes and ears to the needs of others because I want more for myself.
> I repent of allowing the material blessings You have given to deceive me into thinking I don't need You.

I repent of living as though material wealth will
bring happiness.

I repent of being consumed with worry over my
financial, material needs as though You are not
sufficient for all things.

I choose to give You all that I have, not just 10 percent. I trust You to give me, in return, my next breath and
to supply not everything I want but everything I need.
Reveal to me the immense debt I owe You so I can sincerely acknowledge it, live to repay it, and forgive others
as You have forgiven me. I ask that You open my eyes to
the spiritual as well as the material needs of others and use
me to act on Your behalf to meet those needs. I ask for a
fresh vision of Your power and wealth so I would hold
loosely my material blessings, choosing to be content with
or without them, as I look forward to my reward in
Heaven. I ask that You give me courage to see, believe in,
and live in the light of eternity so I resist temptation and
instead abandon myself to Your will.

For the glory of Your great name—*Jesus,*
Amen.

It is such a comfort
to drop the tangles of life
into God's hands
and leave them there.

—L. B. Cowman

A Prayer to the Eternal, Unchanging God

UNCHANGING ONE,
I worship You, the eternal I AM.[1] In a world that is always changing and undulating like the waves of a stormy sea, You never change. You are ever present and always relevant because You are always current. You are never the I Was or the I Will Be. I am confident that Your greatness and power are the same today as they were yesterday—in Creation, in the Exodus, in the Cross, in the Resurrection, in the Ascension, on the Day of Pentecost—and they will be the same at the end of time. You are I AM. And Your standards are high. You still demand holiness of Your people. You still require us "to act justly and to love mercy and to walk humbly" with You.[2]

I confess that I have fallen short of Your perfect standard. I have often failed to live in justice, in mercy, in humility.

How thankful I am to be safe from Your wrath and judgment, under the blood of I AM, Your Lamb, that is smeared on the doorposts of my heart.[3] What joy that I can approach You in prayer, confident You will receive me! You will listen. You will answer. Because the eternal I AM has risen from the dead! He is alive! He has ascended into Heaven! He sits at Your right hand! And He now lives to pray for Your followers even at this moment as I pray to You![4] He is the ruling, reigning, soon-to-return King of kings and Lord of lords. The Lamb upon the throne.

I come to You in His name—*Jesus.* I ask You to be my Refuge and Fortress. Cover me and be with me in times of trouble. Command Your angels to guard and keep me in all my ways.[5] You are a great prayer-hearing, prayer-answering, covenant-keeping, miracle-working God. Hear my prayer! Rise up, great Lion of Judah, so all the nations of the earth may know that You alone are God.

For the glory of Your great name! *Jesus.*

Amen.

Personal Prayer

God is our refuge and strength,
an ever present help in trouble.
Therefore we will not fear, though the
    earth give way
and the mountains fall into the heart of
    the sea,
though its waters roar and foam
and the mountains quake with their
    surging. . . .

The LORD Almighty is with us;
the God of Jacob is our fortress.

—Psalm 46:1–3, 7

A Prayer to the Rock of Our Salvation

R OCK OF AGES,
      We worship You, Elohim, the Strong One. You
were in the beginning. You will be at the end. You always
have been and You always will be. You are the Creator,
who brought forth something out of nothing, who formed
man from dust, who turns darkness into light, who makes
the world turn, who sustains all things by Your powerful
word.[1]

> When the nations rage and the people imagine a
>   vain thing . . .
> When the rulers take a stand and gather together
>   against the Lord . . . [2]
> When the earth gives way . . .
> When the mountains fall into the midst of the
>   sea . . .
> When the waters roar and foam . . .
> When nations are in uproar and kingdoms fall . . .

When everything that is familiar unravels . . . [3]

You are the Rock on which we stand![4] You are
   our Stronghold. We take refuge in You. We hide
   ourselves in You. We worship You alone.

And today we confess our deep need for You.

O God, our Help in ages past, we ask You to inter-
vene on our behalf. As we plunge into spiritual and moral
darkness, we ask You to be our Light. As political, social,
racial, financial, and environmental storms rage all around
us, be our Anchor. As we face terrorism's threat and vows
of annihilation from our enemies, be our Shield. When
there are wars and rumors of wars,[5] be our Peace. In our
weakness, be our Strength. As we grieve over lost free-
doms and lost futures and lost values and lost loved ones,
be our Comfort. In our despair over our lack of moral
leadership, be our Hope. In our confusion when truth is
exchanged for a lie, be our Wisdom.

In these days of desperation and confusion, we look to
You and You alone.

In the strong name of Jesus,
Amen.

[It is here in prayer]
that the ineffable secrets are revealed,
not by a momentary illumination,
but in God himself,
where they are all hid.

—Madame Guyon

A Prayer of Worship: God's Personhood

T RIUNE GOD,
        You are magnificent in the greatness of Your
person. I worship You, the Father who loved me so much
that You brought me into existence and then, after my
sin separated me from You, You sent Your own Son to
be my Savior. And I worship You, the Son, who loved
me so much that, at the Father's direction, You rose from
Heaven's throne, took off Your glory robes, descended to
earth, took on the very nature of a servant made in human
likeness, and humbled Yourself, submitting to death on
a cross. Who can imagine the depths of such love? Or
the heights of such love, as the Father then exalted You
to the highest place so that one day, at Your name, every
knee will bow and every tongue will confess that You are
Lord?[1] Praise God! I can hardly wait for that day. In the
meantime, thank You for not leaving me as an orphan.[2]
You have come to me in the third person of the God-

head. I worship You, the Spirit of truth, my Comforter, my Counselor, my Helper—the Holy Spirit, who is Jesus in me.

Please, dear God, I want to know You better today than I did yesterday. And better tomorrow than I know You today. I want to grow in my knowledge of You until my faith becomes sight and I know You fully, even as today You know me.[3] My heart's desire is that on that day You would acknowledge me as Your friend.

I confess that when my health is good, when my bank account is full, when my friends are many, when my name is well regarded, when my family is happy, I tend to drift into complacency. So I thank You for the trials and tribulations, the heartache and hardships, the disease and disappointments, the weakness and sickness, because they all teach me by experience that I need You. Every moment. Every hour. Every day. My awareness of need presses me to lean hard on You, discovering that in my weakness You are strong, in my inadequacy You are more than enough.

Beloved Father, Son, and Holy Spirit, I trust Your wisdom to know exactly what to send my way to keep me leaning on You. You have said You will not give me more than I can bear.[4] Please help me remain faithful to You, focused on You, and fired up about You, until I see You as You are and You see Yourself reflected in me.[5]

For the glory of Your great name—*Jesus,*
Amen.

Personal Prayer

It is in the personal presence of the
    Saviour,
in intercourse with Him,
that faith rises to grasp what at first
    appeared too high.
It is in prayer
that we hold up our desire
to the light of God's Holy Will.
                    —Andrew Murray

A Prayer of Worship: God's Presence

E TERNAL GOD,
When time and space came into being, You were already there.[1] You had no beginning and will have no end. Your presence is invisible yet powerfully evident. We see You forming a man from the dust of the ground, then breathing Your life into him and, through him, into every human since.[2]

We see You as the ultimate Bondage Breaker, delivering Your children from Egyptian taskmasters with miraculous signs and wonders.[3]

We see You making a way when there was no way as You parted the Red Sea so Your children could pass through on dry ground.[4]

We see You breaking down walls in Jericho so the enemy of the Israelites could be defeated.[5]

We see You showing up in the fiery furnace of Babylon

to protect Your children from being burned—or even singed—because of their loyalty to You.[6]

We see You closing the mouths of hungry lions so Your servant could live to bring You glory.[7]

We see You sweeping into a refugee camp on the wings of a storm to change the calling of one man from that of a priest to that of a prophet.[8]

We see You seated on Heaven's throne, fully in charge, at a time of crisis.[9]

And when You invaded time and space—wonder of wonders!—we see You in the manger bed . . . in the carpenter's shop . . . on the hillside in Galilee . . . hanging on the cross . . . rising out of the tomb . . . ascending into Heaven . . . and sitting back down on Heaven's throne changing everything when You came not just to be with us, before us, behind us, under us, or over us—but to live in us![10]

I bow in utter amazement at and absolute worship of who You are, who You have been, and who You always will be. I am so sorry when I question Your commitment to work out Your eternal purposes in my life or in the lives of my family members. I repent of second-guessing You, of thinking that You have lost Your way in this wicked world or that You are no longer involved in human history. What am I thinking? You are the same today as You were yesterday and as You always will be![11]

Help me live daily with eternity in view.
For the glory of Your great name—*Jesus,*
Amen.

Personal Prayer

Sing to God, O kingdoms of the earth,
sing praise to the Lord,
to him who rides the ancient skies above,
who thunders with mighty voice.
Proclaim the power of God,
whose majesty is over Israel,
whose power is in the skies.
You are awesome, O God, in your
    sanctuary;
the God of Israel gives power and strength
    to his people.

Praise be to God!

—Psalm 68:32–35

A Prayer of Worship: God's Power

ALMIGHTY, OMNIPOTENT GOD,
   There is nothing You cannot do. There is nothing You do not know. There is no place where You are not. My faith in You is rooted deep in Your Word, and therefore I know whom I have believed and I am persuaded that You are able to do above and beyond my expectations and comprehension as You work on my behalf.[1] You are able to supply all I need—gifts, strength, resources, support, encouragement, direction, wisdom, and more— in order to be fully obedient as I live to serve for Your pleasure.[2] You are able to guard and keep me when I am tempted to stray or disobey.[3] You are able to save me in ways I am not even aware of as You respond to Christ's continuous prayers on my behalf.[4] You are able to keep all I have committed to You—my family and my ministry, my health and my home, my life and my loved ones—until I see You face to face.[5] You are able to transform me from

glory to glory . . . character to character . . . so that when I see You, I will be like You.[6] You are able to present me before Your throne one day without fault to the praise of Your glory.[7]

I acknowledge that You are able. I am not. You are able, through the power of Your Spirit, not only to change me from glory to glory but also to change those for whom I am praying. You can change a thoughtless and unloving spouse into someone who reflects and honors You. You can change self-centered children into men and women who live for You. You can change a hostile neighbor into a friend. You can change a lost sibling . . . parent . . . friend . . . coworker . . . into someone who acknowledges sin, repents, and turns to You for salvation.

When I pray, keep my eyes focused on You, the One who is able. Forgive me for acting in the Holy Spirit's place by pointing out sin and trying to convict others. Forgive me for my self-righteous judgment that is quick to find fault. Teach me that Your role is to change people from the inside out, whereas my role is to love them while looking for opportunities to highlight Your truth, not my personal standards.

Thank You for the reassurance that You love others more than I do. You are more concerned for them than I am. You long for them to be holy and pleasing in Your sight. That's why You died. And rose from the dead. And ascended to Heaven. And sent Your Spirit down to live within us. And while I pray for others, please, almighty

God, continue to work out Your will in me until I am pleasing to You. Thank You for Your promise that You, who began a good work in me, will carry it on to completion.[8]

For the glory of Your great name—*Jesus,*
Amen.

Blessed are those who are persecuted
    because of righteousness,
for theirs is the kingdom of heaven.

Blessed are you when people insult you,
    persecute you
and falsely say all kinds of evil against you
    because of me.
Rejoice and be glad,
because great is your reward in heaven,
for in the same way
they persecuted the prophets who were
    before you.

—Matthew 5:10–12

A Prayer for the Persecuted

L ION OF JUDAH,
You are God Almighty.[1] Commander of the armies of Heaven.[2] All power and authority in the entire universe has been given to You.[3] The hearts of earthly kings are in Your hand, and You can do with them as You choose.[4] One day You will speak a word and all Your enemies will be no more.[5]

Until that day, why do You allow the heathen to rage? Why do You allow evil to triumph over good? Why do You allow those who wrong Your people to be exalted, admired, promoted? Why do You allow Your people, called by Your name, to be persecuted—beaten, stoned, beheaded, deserted? Why do You allow the righteous to be maligned? Why do You allow Your followers to be impoverished and the wicked to be prosperous?

I cry out to You on behalf of all those who are suffering because of their faith in You. You have promised that

You will fight for Your people.[6] You have promised to tread upon our enemies.[7] You have promised to give us victory through our Lord Jesus Christ.[8] We now hold You to Your word. Do it. Please!

Even as Your people are persecuted, give us a fresh vision of Yourself as You did for John on Patmos.[9] Give us joy in knowing we are experiencing the intimate fellowship of Your suffering.[10] In our weakness, be our Strength. Store up in Heaven a great reward for our suffering brothers and sisters equal to that given to the saints who have gone before us.[11] Pour out Your Spirit on Your people, infusing us with all we need to remain faithful to the end. And keep us standing against the devil's schemes, feet firmly planted on the truth of Your Word.[12]

Above all, I pray that—through the attacks, the false accusations, the arrests, the imprisonments, the slander, the lawsuits, the physical suffering, and the material deprivation—we would keep our eyes fixed on Jesus, "the author and perfecter of our faith, who for the joy set before him endured the cross, scorning its shame, and sat down at the right hand of the throne of God."[13] Grant to us Your power and perseverance to overcome the Enemy by Your blood and our own testimony. Deliver us from clinging to this life so we will refuse to shrink from death, knowing that the best is yet to come.[14]

In the name of the One who understands firsthand the pain of being persecuted yet who overcame and is Himself the Answer to all our "why" questions—*Jesus,*

Amen.

Since we have a great high priest
who has gone through the heavens,
Jesus the Son of God,
let us hold firmly to the faith we profess.
For we do not have a high priest
who is unable to sympathize with our
    weaknesses,
but we have one who has been tempted in
    every way,
just as we are—yet was without sin.
Let us then approach the throne of grace
    with confidence,
so that we may receive mercy and find
    grace to help us in our time of need.

—Hebrews 4:14–16

A Prayer for National Cleansing and Revival

Most Holy God,

In a world of famine, floods, and fire; a world of disease, death, and the disruption of our everyday activities, I choose to look up from my knees. I see You seated on the throne of glory, in control of all things.[1] *All things.* I know that You are a God of mercy, grace, faithfulness, and loving-kindness.[2] So I reject fear and its impact on my life, and I place my faith in You. You have said that Your ears are open to the cry of Your people,[3] that Your eyes are upon us,[4] and that Your arms are long enough to reach us[5] and strong enough to hold us.[6] Hold me now. Quiet my racing heart. Breathe Your Spirit of peace into me to calm the fear and turmoil.

Even as I pray for Your peace, I wonder if the disasters erupting in our nation could be the spark that ignites a spiritual awakening. Are You trying to get our attention? I know that, when it comes to our relationship with You, we desperately need to wake up.

We have legalized defiance against Your institution of marriage; we celebrate relationships that contradict Your instructions; we exterminate life that You created and that bears Your image—for our own convenience; we have become so secularized we don't even acknowledge that You exist, much less reverence or obey You.

You have my attention. Therefore, like the prophet Daniel of old, I turn to You in humility and shame as I confess on behalf of America some of the national sins that come to mind . . . [7]

> I confess national addiction to sex. To money. To pleasure. To entertainment. To pornography. To technology. To drugs. To alcohol. To food. To television. To popularity. To ourselves.
>
> I confess our foolishness in denying You as the one true, living God, our Creator to whom we are accountable, living as though our lives are a cosmic accident with no eternal significance, purpose, or meaning.
>
> I confess our greed that has run up trillions of dollars of national debt.
>
> I confess our arrogance and pride that has led us to think we are sufficient in ourselves.
>
> I confess to believing that our nation's prosperity comes from our own greatness, while refusing to acknowledge that all blessings come from Your hand.

I confess that we depend on our military might and
our weapons systems to protect us from harm
and danger while we deny, defy, and ignore You.

I confess that we have succumbed to the pressure of
pluralism in our desire to be inclusive, honoring
other gods as though You are just one of many.

I confess that we have allowed the material blessings
You have given us to deceive us into thinking we
don't need You.

I confess that we have valued our foolish pursuit of
happiness through wealth and prosperity rather
than treasuring our relationship with You. I confess that we have marginalized truth and main-
streamed lies.

I confess that we have become one nation under
many gods, divided and polarized, with license
to sin and justice that no longer follows the rule
of law.

Holy Spirit of the living God, convict us of the need
to turn from our sin and get right with You.[8]

Lord God, have mercy on us! As we repent of our sin
and return to You, return to us! There is no one like You
to help the powerless against our mighty enemies, be they
visible or invisible. Help us, O Lord our God, for we rely
on You.[9]

Once again, I hold You to the promise you gave to
King Solomon. You said, "When I shut up the heavens so
that there is no rain, or command locusts to devour the
land or send a plague among my people, if my people,

who are called by my name, will humble themselves and pray and seek my face and turn from their wicked ways, then will I hear from heaven and will forgive their sin and will heal their land. Now my eyes will be open and my ears attentive to the prayers."[10]

I hold You to Your word as I plead with You. Hear my prayer. Forgive our sin. Heal our land. I am standing in the gap for our nation.

I pray in the name of the One who is our Deliverer. Our beautiful and only Savior. Lord of the nations. Son of God and Son of man. The living, reigning, soon-to-return Lord of lords and King of kings, Jesus Christ.

In His name and for His glory, I pray,
Amen.

Praise be to the LORD,
for he has heard my cry for mercy.
The LORD is my strength and my shield;
my heart trusts in him, and I am helped.
My heart leaps for joy
and I will give thanks to him in song.

The LORD is the strength of his people,
a fortress of salvation for his anointed
   one.
Save your people and bless your
   inheritance;
be their shepherd and carry them forever.
—Psalm 28:6–9

A Prayer for the People of God

G ENTLE SHEPHERD,[1]
How we love and trust You. You are a right-now God. For such a time as this, we need You, and therefore, we have You. Not only are You the Light that guides us through the darkening and threatening storms of life, but You are also our spiritual GPS.[2] You lead us on the right path and get us to the place where we need to be. One day You will take us safely Home. We trust You completely. You are Jehovah Rohi, the Lord my Shepherd, who takes full responsibility for the welfare of Your people. For our safety. For our provision. You guard the young. You seek the stray. You find the lost. You guide the faithful. You avenge the abused. You defend the weak. You comfort the oppressed. You welcome the prodigal. You heal the sick. You cleanse the dirty. You beautify the barren. You restore the failure. You mend the broken. You

bless the poor. You fill the empty. You clothe the naked. You satisfy the hungry. You elevate the humble. You forgive the sinner.

We confess that we, Your people, the sheep of Your pasture, are constantly going astray. Each of us has turned to our own way and done what we think is right in our own eyes.[3] The wounded and the wounders, the betrayals and the bickering, the pride and the prejudices, the wealth and the wants, have tarnished the reflection of Your beauty that should rest on us as Your body, the church. We have focused on our circumstances and have therefore been defeated. We have focused on others and have therefore been deluded. We have focused on ourselves and have therefore been deceived. We have focused on political policy and have therefore been disappointed. We compare ourselves with others so that our perception of who we really are is distorted. We repent.

With deep shame, we confess that there are people in the world whom You love and for whom You died . . .

who don't want to know You because they
know us.

who reject You because they reject us.

who don't believe You because of what we say and
the way we say it.

who don't know that You love them because we
don't love them.

who don't know that You can give them victory
over sin because we live in defeat.

who are hopeless because we wring our hands in
    despair.

who are terrified of the future because we are
    afraid.

But now we return to You, the Shepherd of our souls.
We humbly, sincerely say to You, "Forgive all our sins and
receive us graciously." You have promised that You will
heal our waywardness and love us freely.[4] We hold You to
Your word as we sincerely come to You. As we humbly
bow before You.

In the name and for the glory of the One who laid
down His life for us as our Good Shepherd—*Jesus,*

    Amen.

Personal Prayer

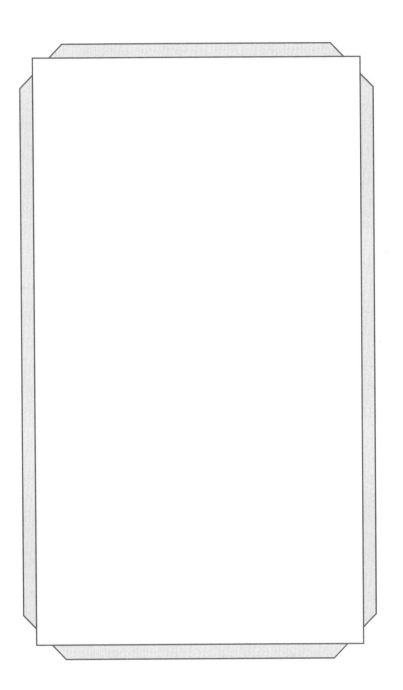

Prayer is the practice of drawing on the
grace of God.
Don't say,
"I will endure this until I can get away
and pray."
Pray *now*—
draw on the grace of God in your
moment of need.

—Oswald Chambers

A Prayer of the Lonely

ALL-KNOWING, ALL-SEEING GOD, I worship You, the One who has eyes to see everything. You see that which is visible and that which is invisible. That which is temporal and that which is eternal. That which is past, that which is present, and that which is yet to come. And You see me. You know me. You know when I sit and when I arise. When I go out and when I come in. When I sleep and when I awake. You know my limitations, and You know my potential. You know my thoughts before they are formed into words. Nothing about me is hidden from You.[1] You are the One who sees me.[2]

And I worship You, the One who is everywhere. There is no place in all the universe where You are not. If I were to ascend to the highest heaven, You would be there. If I were to descend to the lowest depth, You would be there. If I were to settle in the remotest part of the planet, You would guide me and hold me fast. If I were to cower in the darkness, I would not be hidden from You, since darkness is as light to You. I was not hidden from You even when I was being formed in my mother's womb.[3] "You are my hiding place; you . . . surround me with songs of deliverance."[4] You are always with me, and You have promised that You will always be with me.[5] Even to the end of all things.[6] And after the end, You will receive me to glory, where I will see You face to face.[7] Then I will know You even as I am now fully known.[8] And I will be with You. Forever.[9]

So when I am tempted to feel lonely, when there is no one visible to talk to or confide in, when I eat by myself and sleep by myself and walk by myself, give me an awareness of You. Open my mind to Your plan and purpose that give me reason to live another day. Open my ears to Your gentle whispers that reassure me of Your loving, personal attention. Open my eyes to Your blessing upon blessing that fills me with joy. Open my heart to Your love that lifts and carries me beyond myself. Draw me closer to Your heart as I read my Bible and spend time in prayer. Keep me focused not just on the facts and theology and prophecy of Your Word but on You.

Then give me opportunities to encourage others who may feel lonely: widows and orphans, teenagers and single parents, divorcées and singles, CEOs and salesclerks, prisoners and soldiers, the elderly and the sick. Use me to demonstrate the truth that while we may feel lonely, we are never alone. Because we have You and You have us.

In the name of the One who is right here, right now— *Jesus,*

Amen.

Prayer does not fit us for the greater
    works;
prayer *is* the greater work. . . .
Prayer is the battle.

                              —Oswald Chambers

A Prayer for Victory in Battle

ALMIGHTY WARRIOR, LION OF JUDAH, CAPTAIN of Heaven's Armies,

Day and night, forever and ever, eternity will not be long enough to worship You. I love You and adore You. I swear my allegiance to You and You alone amid the battles of daily life—the battle against temptation, the battle for truth. I know that the real enemy is Satan. The devil. The dragon. That old serpent who has led the whole world astray for millennia. And at his side are all the fallen angels—his demons, spiritual forces of evil, principalities and powers.

I ask You to open my eyes to the invisible realm. Tear away the veil of deception, and expose the mesmerizing spirit of the Enemy. Show me Your truth, which Satan twists with his counterfeit wisdom. Give me discernment to detect . . .

his lies in contrast to Your truth,

his suggestions in contrast to Your commands,

his temptations in contrast to Your promises,

his destruction in contrast to Your salvation,

his pleasures that are fleeting,

his plans that are failing,

his purposes that are futile, and

his position that is fraudulent.

Thank You that You have not left Your people defenseless for the battle. Since "our struggle is not against flesh and blood, but against the rulers, against the authorities, against the powers of this dark world and against the spiritual forces of evil in the heavenly realms,"[1] the battle will be won not by our might or by our power but by Your Spirit, who lives within us.[2]

I pray in the name of the Rider on the white horse, whose name is Faithful and True, who one day will return, followed by the armies of Heaven. I pray in the name of the One with eyes of blazing fire, who judges and makes war justly.[3] I pray in the name of the victorious Warrior, who one day will vanquish Satan and remove all evil, rebellion, hatred, injustice, and lies from this planet. I pray in the name of Jesus that You will grant Your people—that You will grant me—victory this day.

In His name—*Jesus*—and for His glory,

Amen.

Personal Prayer

The LORD will lay bare his holy arm
in the sight of all the nations,
and all the ends of the earth will see
the salvation of our God.

—Isaiah 52:10

A Prayer for Deliverance

LORD GOD,

You are *Jehovah Nissi,* the Lord our Banner. At the sound of Your name and at the sight of You, our Battle Standard, the Enemy panics. Strongholds fall. Demons flee. The earth trembles. Heaven is moved. My hands are lifted toward Your throne, and I shout Your name: *Elohim,* God; *Yahweh,* the Lord; *Jehovah Shalom,* the Lord our Peace; *El Elyon,* God Most High; *Jehovah Rohi,* the Lord our Shepherd; *Jehovah Rapha,* the Lord our Healer; *Jehovah Jireh,* the Lord our Provider; *El Roi,* the God who sees me; *El Shaddai,* God Almighty.

I come to You now because the enemy forces have come in like a flood. I lift up the banner of Your name against them.[1] I lift up the Spirit of truth against the lies that too often permeate my thinking and decisions and discussion, undermining my loyalty to You.

I confess and repent of any sin that would give the Enemy entrance into my heart or mind or body.

I repent of . . .

any pride, evidenced in a "me first" mentality.

any envy when others receive more recognition and praise.

a critical spirit that can overtake my thoughts and conversations, demanding that others measure up to my standards.

saying things that are not the whole truth in order to impress others.

stretching the truth, excusing "white lies," as though there are good lies and bad lies.

any hypocrisy—pretending to be something I am not.

any frustration that causes me to lose patience and speak crossly.

I'm sorry.

I confess there have been times when I have lost control of my emotions, thoughts, and words and have left verbal wounds on the hearts of those around me.

I'm so sorry.

I ask You to cleanse me. Remove any sin or spiritual weakness by which the Enemy may gain access to my life. Saturate me in Your Spirit, in Yourself—Your holiness, purity, righteousness, justice, power, mercy, grace, truth, and love. Cover me with Your blood. Give me courage to stand firm against the Enemy, knowing that, through the shed blood of Jesus Christ, You have already won the victory. "Power and might are in your hand, and no one can withstand you."[2] Hear me, O Lord, as I cry out to You.

Help me trust in Your deliverance as I lift up the banner of Your name—*Jesus.*

Amen.

Personal Prayer

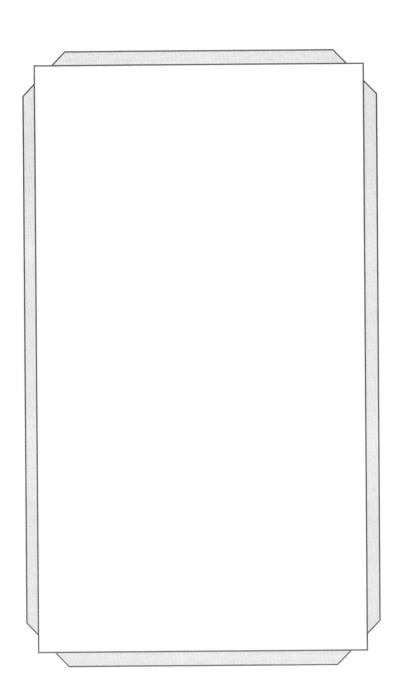

I don't believe
that there is such a thing
in the history of God's kingdom
as a right prayer offered in the right spirit
that is forever left unanswered.

—Theodore L. Cuyler

A Prayer for the Salvation of Family Members

ABBA, FATHER,
  I worship You, Immanuel,[1] God with us. You—Elohim, El Elyon, I AM, Adonai, Jehovah—became flesh and made Your dwelling among us.[2] Who could have imagined the love that devised redemption's plan? You left Heaven's throne, confined Yourself to a woman's womb for nine months, and submitted to the human birth process, entering time and space in order to be with us! And You did this when we were still in our sin and rebellion against You. Because You love us! You have said we are no longer Your servants but Your friends.[3] When we receive You by faith, believing on Your name, we are born into Your family. We have the right to be called Your children and to call You Abba.[4]

  The reality of Your royal, divine Son being born into an ordinary human family reminds me of Your desire to come into my family. I confess that I have failed to intercede for the souls of loved ones, not praying for them or warning them that they are destined for hell if they don't put their faith in Jesus. I have allowed my fear of offending them to override my love for the gospel. I confess that I have not really demonstrated love when I have applauded their financial success or public fame or career position as though that is more important than their spiritual condition and development. I confess that at times I have behaved as if keeping the peace were more important than speaking the truth. Or as if being accepted by family were more important than adhering to Your principles and reflecting Your holiness. I'm sorry.

Now, with my heart bowed before the cross, I intercede for my family. Abba, Father, I ask You to bring every member of my extended family to a saving knowledge of Jesus before judgment comes, either at Your return or at their deaths. I will refrain from giving You suggestions on how to do this, but I ask You to save my loved ones. Snatch them from the fire. Drag them out of their sin. O God of mercy, I cannot bear the thought of going to Heaven without them. I give You permission to do whatever it takes to get them there.

In the meantime, would You please use me to point someone else's family to salvation? Give me sensitivity to Your Spirit so that I follow His lead, going where He directs, speaking to whomever He brings across my path, saying what He brings to my mind. Give me the joy of being the answer to someone else's prayer by leading that person's loved ones to trust in Jesus.

Gracious Father, I pray this in the name of Your Son and my Savior, whose sacrifice on the cross has brought me into Your family—*Jesus.*

Amen.

All real prayer

is simply asking that God's will may be
    done,

which will is sure to be done. . . .

Nothing lies beyond the reach of prayer

except that which lies outside

the pure, kind, and saving will of God.

—Samuel Cox

A Prayer of Thanksgiving for the Power of the Cross

BELOVED SON OF THE FATHER,
    Thank You for the Cross. Thank You that Your blood is just as powerful today as it was two thousand years ago when the first drop was shed on Calvary. Thank You that through Your blood we have redemption and the forgiveness of our sins.¹ Thank You that You cleanse us of all unrighteousness when we use the same labels for sin that You do, as we humbly and honestly confess our sins to You.²

We fall at the foot of the cross and repent of every sin that made Your death necessary. Every sin that even now is provoking Your displeasure.

    I confess _____ (fill in the blank with any sin that comes to mind).
    Thank You that our every sin is nailed to the cross and we no longer bear its penalty or guilt.

Thank You that You invite forgiven sinners to draw near to You with sincere hearts in full assurance of faith.[3]

Thank You that we can ask according to Your will, knowing that You hear us.[4]

We ask that You would increase within us a magnificent obsession to know You in a personal, intimate, loving relationship. Give us spirits that reject religion, that do not settle for knowing about You or going through the motions of rituals and traditions and ceremonies. Lead us to embrace You fully at any cost. Open the eyes of our hearts so we might live with eternity in view. Keep Heaven continuously on our minds so this world loses its appeal. Strengthen the ties of faith that bind us first to You, then to one another. Fill us with Your power so we overcome our addictions, bad habits, temptations, and half-hearted discipleship. Give us miracles in answer to prayer. Not for our own credit, but so the world may know that our God is God and that You answer the prayers of Your people when they cry out to You. Take us back to Your Word. Give us ears to hear Your voice. Drive us to our knees in prayer. Confront us with the seriousness of the times in which we are living. Wake us up! Don't let us be caught by surprise at the end. Compel us to go back to the cross and lead others there by our own example. Before it's too late.

With thankfulness for the salvation and forgiveness that are ours through the Cross, we pray in the name of Your Son and our Savior—*Jesus.*

Amen.

How beautiful on the mountains

are the feet of those who bring good news,

who proclaim peace,

who bring good tidings,

who proclaim salvation,

who say to Zion,

"Your God reigns!"

—Isaiah 52:7

A Prayer to Make a Difference in a Hurting World

Blessed Heavenly Father,
   All Your promises are trustworthy. All life's
questions are answered in You. You are the Sustainer of
all things. I worship You, the Fountainhead of all blessing,
the Source of all life, the Wellspring of wisdom, the Key
to knowledge, the Foundation of faith, the Doorway to
glory. I worship You, the One who supplies strength to the
weary, increases power to the faint, and offers escape to
the tempted.[1] I worship You, the One who sympathizes
with the hurting, shields the defenseless, enriches the
poor, sustains the helpless, and shelters the homeless. You
give purpose to the aimless, comfort to the lonely, fruit to
the barren, beauty to the meek, a future to the hopeless,
and life to the lifeless!

   Lord, I confess that I too often overlook the people
who need Your love and healing. Consumed with myself
and my schedule, I don't make time to listen for Your lead-

ing and to watch for opportunities to give Jesus to those around me. Forgive me, Father.

In a world of lonely, frightened people, give me a heart that is broken for the things that break Yours. Give me compassion for a lost and dying world, for people You love. Give me an unquenchable love for Your gospel, for Your Son, for Your Word, for You. Use me to make an eternal difference in the lives of people all around me. I humbly, boldly ask that You give me the attention of my friends, neighbors, coworkers, classmates, even my enemies, so that they see my example and . . .

want to know You because they know me.

place their faith in You because I am trustworthy.

believe You because of what I say and the way
I say it.

know that You love them, because I love them.

know that You can give them victory over sin, because my life demonstrates it.

have hope because I am so genuinely confident.

go to You for freedom from the power of sin because I speak the truth in love.

have peace because I am not afraid.

look to You as the solution for what's wrong, because I am looking to You.

Now I ask You to grow me into someone who reflects You in all I say and do.

For the glory of Your name—*Jesus,*
Amen.

Personal Prayer

Every life that would be strong
must have its Holy of Holies
into which only God enters.
                    —L. B. Cowman

A Prayer of Dependence on God's Power and Authority

L ord Jesus Christ,
I worship You, the Lamb who was slain but who is now enthroned at the center of the universe as the King of kings and the Lord of lords, soon to return in power and glory. You are Jesus, who calmed the stormy seas with just a word.[1] You turned water into wine.[2] You created sight in a man born blind.[3] You raised the dead.[4] You are the same One who set the boundaries for the oceans.[5] The same One who hung the stars in space and calls them all by name.[6] The same One who strides the winds of the earth so the clouds are the dust of Your feet.[7]

I choose to surrender my life to Your power and authority in utter moment-by-moment dependence on Your moment-by-moment control. I ask You to manifest Your power and keep my attention fixed on You, no matter what happens in the world around me. I ask that Your presence would permeate my life in such a way that others would be drawn to You. That Your power in my life would be so evident that evil spirits flee. That Your strong arm would be around me and under me, carrying me when I am weak, shielding me when I'm attacked, helping me up when I fall, holding me close to Your heart.

I humbly ask all this for the glory of Your great name—*Jesus.*

Amen.

Is any one of you in trouble?
He should pray.
Is anyone happy?
Let him sing songs of praise.
Is any one of you sick?
He should call the elders of the church
to pray over him and anoint him with oil
in the name of the Lord.
And the prayer offered in faith
will make the sick person well;
the Lord will raise him up.
If he has sinned,
he will be forgiven.
Therefore confess your sins to each other
and pray for each other so that you may
    be healed.
The prayer of a righteous man
is powerful and effective.

—James 5:13–16

A Prayer of Contrition

GREAT AND AWESOME GOD,
Your right hand, O Lord, is majestic in power. And in the greatness of Your excellence, You overthrow those who rise against You; You send forth Your burning anger, and it consumes them as chaff.[1] While You are slow to anger and great in power, You will not at all acquit the wicked.[2] You have Your way in the whirlwind and in the storm. The clouds are the dust of Your feet.[3]

We pray with contrite spirits. We are ashamed and embarrassed to lift our faces to You, for our iniquities have risen above our heads and our guilt has grown even to the heavens. So now, our God, what shall we say?[4]

"We have sinned and done wrong. We have been wicked and have rebelled."[5]

We have suppressed the truth that we were created by You and for You and have exchanged it for the lie that we are masters of our own fates.[6]

We confess to religious indifference that gives lip service to You but lacks sincere faith so that we live and make decisions as practical atheists—as though You do not exist.

We confess to generational hatred and racial prejudice that are like a disease, perpetuating divisiveness, destruction, and turmoil.

You are merciful and forgiving, even though we have rebelled against You. So this day we come to You with humble, contrite spirits to confess our sin and ask for Your mercy. We seek Your forgiveness. Open our eyes to see You for who You truly are. Don't let us remain blinded by religiosity and self-interest. We ask You to show up in great power, giving us supernatural strength to pursue justice, to remember mercy, to walk humbly with You.[7] We ask that You would shatter the Enemy so victory will be won not by our might nor by our power but by Your Spirit.[8]

In the glorious name of Jesus, who died to make us free,

Amen.

Personal Prayer

The Christian
on his knees
sees more
than the philosopher on tiptoe.
—Dwight L. Moody

A Prayer for True Wisdom

GOD ONLY WISE,[1]
I worship You, Lord Jesus, for You are the incarnation of God's wisdom.[2] Your judgments are un-searchable. Your ways are past finding out. Your thoughts are higher than ours.[3] Your plans never include a mistake. There are no accidents as You carry out Your purpose. You never have to second-guess what You have done or what You plan to do. You are right—all the time, in every way.

I confess my attitude of familiarity that tends to re-place a reverential fear of You, which is the beginning of wisdom.[4] I acknowledge the foolishness of denying that You are the one true, living God, the Creator to whom all of us are accountable. I refuse to live as though my life is a cosmic accident with no eternal significance, pur-pose, or meaning. I choose to trust in You instead of leaning on my own understanding.[5] I choose to look to

You in prayer instead of placing my trust in politics or government programs or family assistance. I repent of succumbing at times to conventional wisdom and popular opinion instead of seeking You first and asking You what I should do.

I choose to honor You, the source of all life, living with reverential fear of and respect for You and conducting my life according to Your principles and values as given in Your Word. I need Your wisdom every hour of every day for decisions, for direction, for discernment, for counsel that I impart to others, and for a myriad of other things. You have promised that if I ask You for wisdom, You will give it to me in generous amounts without making me feel guilty for having none of my own.[6] So I am asking You now for Your true wisdom.

I ask that as I look to You for wisdom, my example would be contagious and others would observe that living according to Your wisdom works. I ask that You open my spiritual eyes to see the foolishness of following the crowd or compromising eternal Truth because it is not politically correct or succumbing to peer pressure in order to be more accepted or trying to blend into the culture so as not to invite criticism or ostracism. Lord God, I don't want to waste my life! I ask that You open my eyes to recognize the lies that deny the truth and the spin that distorts the truth so that counterfeit wisdom, which is really foolishness, has no hiding place. I ask that You generously give me wisdom from on high and let my life, my words, my priorities effectively present You and Your gospel to all those I encounter.

I humbly ask this for the glory of Your great name— *Jesus.*

Amen.

Prayer is an earnest and familiar talking
     with God,
to whom we declare our miseries,
whose support and help we implore
     and desire in our adversities,
and whom we laud and praise for our
     benefits received.

—John Knox

A Prayer for True Security and Prosperity

L ord Jesus Christ,
    We worship You, the Almighty—our breath-
taking and all-powerful Lord. You measure the waters in
the hollow of Your hand. You weigh the mountains on
scales. You stretch out the heavens like a curtain.[1] Your
immensity is impossible for us to comprehend. You make
a way when there is no way. You alone have the strength
to establish, preserve, and prosper us. We need You!

> We repent of our pride that has led us to think we
> are sufficient in ourselves.
>
> We repent of believing that our prosperity is of our
> own making while refusing to acknowledge that
> all blessings come from Your hand.
>
> We repent of looking to the president or to a pastor
> or to a priest or to a government agency for the
> help we need before we look to You.

We repent of depending on our military or our weapons for protection and security while denying, defying, and ignoring You.

We choose to rely on You and to pray without ceasing.[2]

We ask that You strengthen Your people with might on the inside—that You make one of us as mighty as a thousand.[3]

We ask that You give us deep convictions regarding the truth of who You are and what You have said—and the courage to stand up and speak out for it.

We ask that as we live in total dependence on Your strength, You give us experiences of Your miraculous enabling so that we boast of our own weaknesses.[4]

We ask that You give us blessed assurance that You are greater than the evil in the world—and grant us the conviction to stand against that evil.[5]

Remind us that Your love is stronger than hate and that the light of Your truth will never be overcome by the darkness, so that we lovingly and boldly proclaim that victory has been won! Because Jesus saves!

I humbly ask for the glory of Your great name—*Jesus.* Amen.

Personal Prayer

The surrender to God to seek His glory,
and the expectation that He will show
    His glory in hearing us,
are one at root:
He that seeks God's glory will see it
in the answer to his prayer.

—Andrew Murray

A Prayer to Live Boldly for God's Glory

Enthroned Lord Jesus,[1]
I worship You, the One whose name is above every name. There is no one like You. You are the One who sits on the throne at the center of the universe. You are the Creator, the Messiah, the Redeemer of Israel, the Savior of the world, the Hope of the ages. You alone are able to rule the world and fulfill the Father's purpose for the human race, yet You humbled Yourself to the point of death on the cross that You might be the ransom for our sin.[2] Your greatness makes me acutely aware of my smallness and leads me to repentance.

> I repent of caring more about my own reputation than Yours.
> I repent of giving You my leftover money, my leftover time, and even my leftover love, implying You are second best.

I repent of priorities, actions, and decisions that
  exalt myself, my friends, my family, other people,
  and even my bank account above You.
I repent of compromising the gospel to give lip
  service to tolerance and inclusion.
I repent of claiming to honor You when my heart is
  far from You.
I repent of robbing You of the honor due Your
  name.

I choose to seek Your kingdom and Your righteousness before all else, placing You alone on the throne of
my heart. I count my life as nothing that You might be
everything. I abandon myself to Your will. I regret that I
have only one life to live for Your glory and Your honor
alone. I choose to publicly declare—in honor of Your
name—that all have sinned, that there is forgiveness of
sin at the cross, that there is no other way to the Father
but through You, that eternal life is found through faith
in You alone. I ask that as I honor You, You would honor
me with Your favor and the goodwill of my neighbors
and coworkers; that even those who don't believe in You
will respect Your name because of the way I honor it. I ask
that as Your name is lifted up, dark spirits would flee.
I ask that Your name would be a strong tower to those
who take refuge in You.[3]

  I humbly ask in Your name—*Jesus,*
  Amen.

While I was speaking and praying,
confessing my sin and the sin of my
     people . . .
and making my request to the LORD my
     God . . .
while I was still in prayer,
Gabriel . . . said to me, . . .
"As soon as you began to pray, an answer
     was given,
which I have come to tell you,
for you are highly esteemed."

—Daniel 9:20–23

A Prayer for Strength to Stand

L IVING WORD,
I worship You, the supreme Logos of the universe. You are the outward expression and revelation of the mind and will that order and give meaning to everything. You are the glorious, almighty Creator, who entered and became part of Your creation. How stunning that You came to those You created, to those who should have recognized You, received You, bowed down before You—but who instead rejected You.[1] I worship You for Your great love that persevered through the rejection because of the joy that awaited You.[2] How almost inconceivable it is to think that we are Your joy!

Help me live in such a way that I am a joy to You. I recognize You as the Light of the world, not just the Light for any one people group.[3] Your name is above all names, the only name by which we can be saved.[4] By which I am saved. You are God's Lamb sacrificed for my sin.[5] You are the risen Lord, who will soon return to rule the world as King of kings. I bow down now in joyful, humble surrender to You, declaring my allegiance.

As I seek to bring delight to You, I will live according to Your Word, Your truth. My worldview will be dictated by what You say, not by popular opinion or cultural norms. I believe that You created everything, because You said so.[6] So I reject evolution because You have said that everything You created was created after its kind.[7] While there can be great diversity within a species, there is no crossover between species. I believe there are only two genders, because You have said that You created us male and female.[8] I believe in marriage between one man and one woman because You said, "For this reason a man will leave his father and mother and be united to his wife, and they will become one flesh."[9] I believe all human life is precious, because You said we are created in Your image.[10] I believe in the value of unborn life because You have said that "you created my inmost being; you knit me together in my mother's womb."[11]

Give me the courage, the strength, the fortitude to live by Your Word, even if all those around me buy into the Enemy's lies. Your Word is truth. Help me apply it to the issues of our day, then stand on it. And when the nations crumble and the people imagine a vain thing, I will stand on a foundation that remains firm.[12] Immovable. Eternal. Because I'm standing on the Rock.[13]

As I live according to Your Word, let me reflect Your values to those who watch me so they may discover that standing on Your Word is the most secure place they can be! Call out for Yourself a remnant of followers who will stand firm on the truth, and having done all we can do to impart it to others, may we still stand even if we are the last ones to do so.

I pray this in the name of the One who is truth—*Jesus, the Living Word.*

Amen.

Personal Prayer

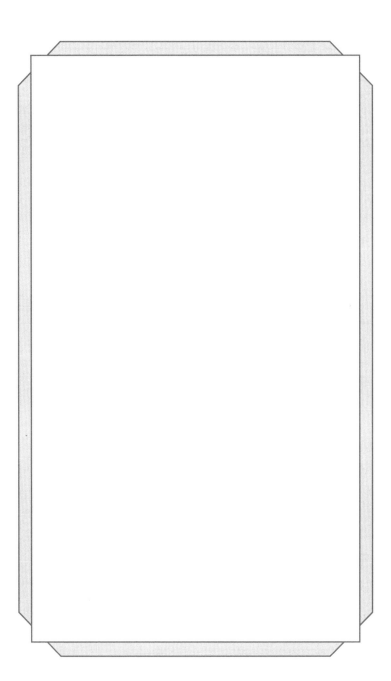

"Even now," declares the LORD,
"return to me with all your heart,
with fasting and weeping and mourning."

Rend your heart
and not your garments.
Return to the LORD your God,
for he is gracious and compassionate,
slow to anger and abounding in love,
and he relents from sending calamity.

—Joel 2:12–13

A Prayer of Confession and Repentance

COVENANT-MAKING, COVENANT-KEEPING GOD,
Your mercy endures forever. Your love endures forever.[1] Your Word endures forever. Your faithfulness is to all generations.[2] You are the Rock that does not move. You are for us. You have chosen us. You have saved us. You have given us freely, graciously "everything we need for life and godliness."[3] From the fullness of Your grace, You have poured out on us one blessing after another.[4]

Yet we have failed to respond to Your generosity, blessings, and mercy as we should.

We confess to You our ingratitude. We have not been truly thankful to You for the blessings You have given us before and after salvation. Instead, we have given ourselves credit for many of the blessings that come from Your hand.

We repent.

We confess that we've allowed our love for You to grow cold. We have lost our passionate first love for You. Instead, we give our love to our bank accounts, our sports teams, our pleasures, our careers, other people, or even to ourselves.

We repent.

We confess our neglect of Your Word, the Bible. We spend more time reading blogs, online news, the latest bestselling novel, business periodicals, or even owner's manuals for our newest tech toys than we do reading Your Word.

We repent.

We confess our unbelief. In reality, we think Your promises are for others or for another day. We don't think they actually work for us now. And thus we call You a liar.

We repent.

We confess our prayerlessness. We ask others to pray for us, but we don't pray for ourselves. We day-dream, fantasize, and indulge in wishful thinking and call it "prayer." Then we blame You when You don't answer.

We repent.

We confess our love of the world and material things. We complain about or resent the fact that we owe You a minimum of 10 percent of our income. So we don't give it to You.

We repent.

We confess that we have robbed You of the honor due You. We give You the leftovers of our time, thoughts, emotions, money. We waste time on things that have no eternal value. We exercise our God-given gifts and talents for a fee. We are willing to do for a price what we will not do freely for You.

We repent.

Holy Lord, with tears on our faces and shame in our hearts, we sincerely, courageously rend our hearts.[5] We repent of our sin. Not only do we name it for what it is in Your sight, but we also turn away from it. We claim Your promise of forgiveness of sin through Your blood. We claim Your promise that if we confess our sins, You will be faithful and just to forgive us and purify us.[6]

Thank You for Your forgiveness. Thank You for the blood that washes us clean. Thank You that our tears were on Your face. Thank You that as our High Priest You understand firsthand our human weaknesses.[7] Thank You that although You were sinless, You became sin for us that we might be right with You.[8]

We bow before You in humble gratitude.

In Jesus's name,

Amen.

This is the message
we have heard from him and declare to
    you:
God is light;
in him there is no darkness at all.
If we claim to have fellowship with him
yet walk in the darkness,
we lie and do not live by the truth.
But if we walk in the light,
as he is in the light,
we have fellowship with one another,
and the blood of Jesus, his Son,
purifies us from every sin.

—1 John 1:5–7

A Prayer for Restored Beauty in the Body of Christ

L IVING HEAD,[1]
     We worship You, our true God in homespun and sandals, come down to perfectly reveal to us the character of the Father. When we want to know what God is like, we can look at You. When we want to know what's in His heart, we can look at You. When we want to know what God thinks about us, we can look at You. You illuminate the darkness of our circumstances and the chaotic confusion of our world, giving us hope for the future. You are the marvelous, everlasting, and all-powerful Light that shines in our hearts that we might walk no longer in the darkness of deception, fear, ignorance, and evil but in Your love and the light of Your glory. And in Your light, we see ourselves . . .

    We have tarnished Your glory with our bitterness,
       meanness, unforgiveness, pride, unkindness,

rudeness, self-righteousness, and with other sins that make people think less of You.

We have given others the impression that You tolerate sin in us, because we do.

We have hidden Your glory in our denominational loyalty, which can lead to divisiveness and exclusiveness. In doing so, we have made others feel they are on the periphery of Your inner circle, alienated from You.

We have lashed out to wound others when we've been wounded and so perpetuate the cycle of pain within Your body, diminishing the radiance of Your unconditional love, mercy, and grace.

We have run from Your marvelous light back into dark areas of painful memories, old habits, forbidden relationships, and seductive pleasures.

We have given You glory while taking a 10 percent commission for ourselves.

We are so deeply sorry.

We choose to give You all the glory and to reflect Your glory accurately and winsomely, through the powerful presence of Your Spirit within us, so that others are irresistibly drawn to You. We ask, as we turn away from our sin, that You cleanse us and fill us with Yourself so that Your church is filled with Your glory. We ask that Your church—Your body—once again be the light of the world, a city on a hill that cannot be hidden, beckoning the lost to come home to You.[2] We ask that the conduct and character of each one of us as members of Your body would make others want to know You, to love You, and to put their trust in You, our living Head.[3]

We humbly ask for the glory of Your great name— *Jesus,*

Amen.

The secret prayer chamber

is

a bloody battleground.

—Ole Hallesby

A Prayer to Overcome Evil with Good

L ORD JESUS CHRIST,
We praise You, the One who declares Your
greatness and glory in creation. The heavens, pitched like
a tent for the sun, speak of Your vastness.[1] The sun, unfail-
ingly rising and setting, speaks of Your faithfulness. The
billions of stars, sparkling like diamonds in the dark ex-
panse of the night sky, reveal Your vast, personal knowledge, as You call each one by name.[2] The boundaries that
You set for the sea speak of Your laws that are for our
good.[3] The sparrows that You see fall and the lilies that
You clothe point to Your compassionate, individualized
attention.[4]

We praise You, our Creator, for we are wonderfully
and fearfully made in Your image, with a capacity to know
You in a personal relationship. You know our thoughts
before they become words. You numbered our days and
recorded them before we were born. You know when we

go out and when we come in. When we rise and when we lie down.[5] We worship You, the Lamb who was slain, who alone is worthy of all praise. Our hearts yearn for the day when we will gather around Your throne, seeing with our own eyes the angels and people whose numbers are too great to count and hearing with our own ears the multitude crying out in such unity that they sound like one loud voice: "Worthy is the Lamb, who was slain, to receive power and wealth and wisdom and strength and honor and glory and praise!"[6] The entire universe will roar in praise of You!

We hear the hiss of that old serpent, the devil, in the lies, blasphemies, and profanities that bombard our ears. With tactics designed to undermine our trust in You, the supreme Lord of the universe, he appears to us as an angel of light, seeking to deceive, weaken, distract, divide, devour, and ultimately destroy us.[7]

But no more. Not today.

On this day, as Your mighty army, in the name of our Lord Jesus Christ, the Lion of Judah, the Captain of the Lord's host, we come against the devil, his demons, and all those he is using for his evil purposes. We command the evil spirits to be bound, confused, and powerless. We command that the evil the Enemy is plotting against Your people would be thwarted and that all the Enemy intends for us will fall back on him. We lift high the cross as our battle standard. Protect and deliver us from evil, we earnestly pray. Give us confidence that more are those who are with us than those who are with them.[8] That greater are You within us than any evil one who is in our world.[9] Use us to rescue those who are in the Enemy's grip, to snatch them from the fire. Most holy Father, we ask that Your kingdom come, Your will be done here on earth as it is done there in Heaven.[10] Shine Your light into the deep recesses of our world where the Enemy seems to rule: gulags, killing fields, prisons, religious institutions, covens, brothels, and places too terrible to name. Reveal to us how to resist and overcome evil. Help us strengthen others to stand with us, shoulder to shoulder against it.

We pray in the name of the victorious Lion of Judah— *Jesus.*

Amen.

Personal Prayer

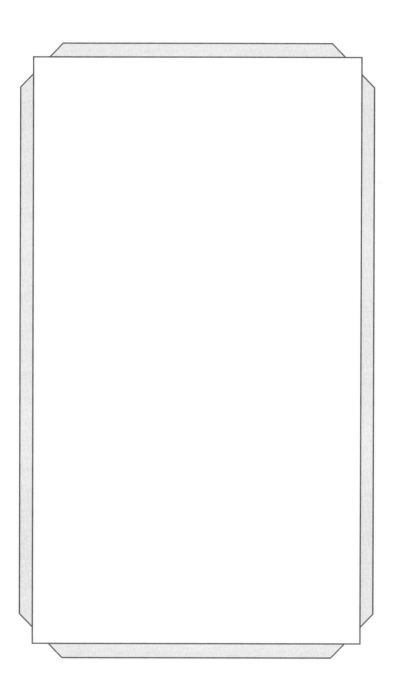

You are the salt of the earth.
But if the salt loses its saltiness,
how can it be made salty again?
It is no longer good for anything,
except to be thrown out and trampled
   by men.

You are the light of the world.
A city on a hill cannot be hidden.
Neither do people light a lamp and put
   it under a bowl.
Instead they put it on its stand,
and it gives light to everyone in the
   house.

—Matthew 5:13–15

A Prayer to Be Salt and Light

F ATHER OF OUR LORD JESUS CHRIST,
We come to You in the name of the One by
whom "all things were created: things in heaven and on
earth, visible and invisible, whether thrones or powers or
rulers or authorities."[1] We come to You in the name of the
Creator, who became our Savior and who has ascended
into Heaven to sit at Your right hand, with all authority
placed under His feet.[2] We come to You humbly yet boldly
because we have been invited to come.[3] We come to You
with confidence because the way has been opened for us
by the blood of Your Son, who sits at Your right hand,
who is in authority over all.[4] We come to You with sincere
hearts in full assurance of faith, knowing that You will receive us, You will listen to us, and You will answer us.[5]
Hear our prayers as we come to You in the name of Jesus.

We confess that we, as Your people—Your church—
have turned away from Your commands and Your Word.

We defend the right to post the Ten Commandments on a courthouse wall, yet we would be hard pressed to name five of them. We cry out for revival yet are too busy to turn to You in prayer and fasting, in confession of and repentance for our sin. We don't declare the whole counsel of Scripture for fear of offending our listeners. We have been ashamed of You and Your Word, unwilling to align ourselves with truth for fear of being misunderstood, despised, marginalized, or rejected by those around us. To our deep shame, the list of our sins seems endless. We are so sorry. Today we repent. We turn away from our sins as we turn and seek Your face.

We humble ourselves and ask that Your name be glorified in and through us. We pray that Your Son would be exalted first in our own hearts, then in our families, churches, and nation. Jesus promised that when He is lifted up on the Cross . . . when the gospel is clearly presented . . . He will draw all people to Himself.[6] So we lift Him up! We present Him as the crucified Savior, the risen Lord. As we do, we boldly ask that You would set our hearts on fire, compelling us to share the good news of Your love for sinners and Your hope for a broken world. Turn the hearts of Your people back to worship, magnifying You so that as people observe us, they will be drawn to You. Use the problems, pressures, and pain; the trials, trouble, and trauma we experience as a showcase for Your glory so that when others see our love, joy, peace, patience, kindness, meekness, and self-control,[7] they will know they are seeing Jesus in us and will want to know

You too. May we, Your people, be bold to speak the mighty name of Jesus.

On this day, we choose to follow Jesus because we want to know Him and the power of His resurrection in our daily lives. We are willing to share even in the fellowship of His sufferings.[8] Raise us up as a body of believers who will be beacons of Your light, heralds of Your good news, demonstrations of Your love, trumpeters of Your truth, ministers of Your comfort, and ambassadors of Your peace. May we be the salt and light You declared us to be.[9] Purify us. Keep us on high alert so that we are unashamed when He comes,[10] ready as a glorious bride without spot or blemish to greet our Bridegroom.[11] Use our expectancy to ignite the hope of others. We choose to redeem the time we have left so we do not waste a moment in inviting all to live with You forever, clearly explaining how they can be assured their names are recorded in the Lamb's book of life.[12]

We boldly ask all this in the name of the One who is coming—*Jesus,*

Amen.

Arise, shine, for your light has come,
and the glory of the LORD rises upon
    you.
See, darkness covers the earth
and thick darkness is over the peoples,
but the LORD rises upon you
and his glory appears over you.
                        —Isaiah 60:1–2

A Prayer for an Outpouring of the Holy Spirit

G OD OF ELIJAH,

You are Lord of lords and King of kings. I worship You, the Alpha and the Omega. The Beginning and the End.[1] Human history began in response to Your powerful Word, and human history, as we know it, will end with Your loud command, with the voice of the archangel, and with the blast of Your trumpet. You will raise to life the dead who placed their faith in You. Then suddenly, in the twinkling of an eye, we, Your people; we, who love and trust You; we, who remain alive on the earth—we will be caught up in the air with You and the risen dead, and we will live forever in our heavenly Home. With You![2] Hallelujah!

In light of this truth, even as I am awed by the magnificence of Your glory, I am compelled to wonder how I have become so self-absorbed. Why is my spirit so often apathetic, even lifeless? Why are my days not absorbed in loving You and obeying You and sharing You with those around me? When did the light of Your truth grow dim and the trumpet call of the gospel become muffled? I acknowledge that one day I will stand before You and give an account for the way I have lived, the words I have spoken, the activities that have consumed my days. I shudder to think of what You would say if I had to stand before You today. And I humbly implore You to accept my confession and repentance.

I long for Your glory to be evident in my life. You are the same One to whom Elijah called on Mount Carmel. Elijah obeyed You when he confronted the evil of his day. He depended on You when he confronted wicked Ahab, king of Israel, and the prophets of Baal, built the altar, then soaked it with water. He expected You to honor his obedience and dependence when he publicly called down fire from Heaven. And the fire fell![3] O God of Elijah! Do it again! You are the great I AM, the One who is the same today as You were yesterday and as You forever will be.[4] I ask You for an outpouring of Your Spirit on my nation, on my church, on my family . . . on me! Send down Your Spirit in Pentecostal fullness! Captivate me with Your love! Rend my heart with deep conviction and sorrow for sin! Revive my heart, filling me with abundant life! Ignite my heart with a pure and holy passion to love You and to live for You and Your glory alone! Then use me to bring revival to the hearts of Your people! And use me, Lord, as a messenger of salvation. Saturate every fiber of my being with Your holiness, purity, righteousness, justice, power, mercy, grace, truth, and love. Saturate me with Yourself. Revive my confidence in You; restore the authenticity of my personal relationship with You. Please.

For the glory of Your great name—*Jesus,*
Amen.

For resurrection-stillness
There is resurrection-power,
And the prayer and praise of trusting
May glorify each hour.

—Emily Steele Elliott

A Prayer to Live for a Greater Purpose

F ATHER GOD,

I come to You in grateful adoration. As the Sovereign of the universe, You exercise kindness, justice, and righteousness.[1] And You have been so good to me. You have poured out Your blessings on me, beginning with the gift of life itself. My every breath comes from You. And then You add blessing upon blessing.

I confess that far too often I take for granted my relationship with You and the gift of Your presence. I don't know You as well as I should, because I don't make time to be with You, to read Your Word, to listen for Your voice, to confide in You, to attend to the nudges of the Holy Spirit.

Today I choose to give You back the life You've given me. I choose to live it for a greater purpose than just my own pleasure. I ask You to make my life a reflection of Your love and holiness and glory. Build my life on a strong foundation of faith in You. And use my moments and my days, Lord, for Your divine purpose and glory. May my words and actions serve to strengthen the faith of others as I look to You for wisdom. For guidance. For protection. For peace. For the power to make a difference in the world around me.

In the name of Jesus, I pray.

Amen.

Personal Prayer

It is not by eloquent sermons
that perishing souls are going to be
reached;
we need the power of God
in order that the blessing may
come down.

—Dwight L. Moody

A Prayer for Future Generations

G OD OF ABRAHAM, ISAAC, AND JACOB,
You have been our dwelling place through-
out the generations.[1] Your faithfulness, Your fame, Your
promises, Your covenant, Your authority, Your glory continue year after year, decade after decade, century after
century, millennium after millennium.[2] You have not
changed since the beginning. Your Word is forever set-
tled.[3] Not one jot or tittle, not one punctuation mark, will
pass away until all is fulfilled.[4] What You say is so. You say
what You mean and mean what You say. You are the foundation on which all life that lasts is built.[5] Fear of You is the
beginning of knowledge.[6] Obedience to You brings blessing. Disobedience to You invites disaster.

As I consider my generation—and the ones that
follow—I am appalled. We are in a spiritual and moral free
fall. A great darkness of lies, unbelief, ignorance, and evil
covers the world. People are living as though You do not

exist. I shudder to think of what future generations will face, the generations of my children and grandchildren. Unless they rebuild the foundation of authentic faith, our nation will crumble. It is crumbling now.

In the midst of political turmoil, racial division, social upheaval, financial uncertainty, virus pandemics, and worldwide chaos, I earnestly pray for my children and grandchildren.

I pray that they would be lights in the thick moral and spiritual darkness.[7]

I pray that they would love Your Word and fully obey You and therefore be blessed in their homes and families, in their businesses and careers, in their neighborhoods and their cities.[8]

I pray that You would fill them with the knowledge of Your will through all spiritual wisdom and understanding.

I pray that they would live lives worthy of You, pleasing You in every way as they bear much eternal fruit so when they see You, they receive Your reward.

I pray that You would give them the Spirit of wisdom and revelation so they grow in their knowledge of and relationship with You and grow in their godly character.

I pray that they would be strengthened with all power according to Your glorious might so they may have great endurance to live in an increasingly godless society.

I pray that they would always be mindful of Your

blessings so they live with joyful gratitude, regardless of the curveballs life throws at them.

I pray that the eyes of their hearts would be enlightened to know the hope of Heaven so they are passionate about living with You then and for You now.

I pray that they would have a rich grasp of the heritage entrusted to them, using it for Your glory and not their own gain.[9]

I pray that they would be filled with Your Spirit and therefore bold in their witness, never ashamed to give testimony about You and Your gospel.[10]

I pray that they would refuse to be enticed by the love of money and material things but would instead pursue righteousness, godliness, faith, love, endurance, and gentleness.[11]

I pray that they would be wise about what is good while being innocent about what is evil.[12]

I pray that they would place a higher value on purity than on popularity.

Redeem my parenting mistakes and failures. Help my children and grandchildren overcome the consequences of my sins. Keep them from falling away from You into sin. I long to see them one day presented before Your glorious presence without fault and with great joy.[13]

On that day, I will humbly bow and worship You for Your goodness, grace, and faithfulness to all generations.

For the glory of Your great name—*Jesus,*
Amen.

How beautiful on the mountains
are the feet of those who bring
   good news,
who proclaim peace,
who bring good tidings,
who proclaim salvation,
who say to Zion,
"Your God reigns!"

—Isaiah 52:7

A Prayer for the Mission-Minded

Savior of the World,

Your love for ruined sinners is incomprehensible. You have ransomed us from the power of sin. You have destroyed the victory of the grave.[1] Through Your death You defeated the one who had the power of death—the devil—releasing us from the fear of death, which had kept us bound all our lives.[2] Through our faith in You, we receive forgiveness of sin, salvation from hell, eternal life, a heavenly Home, and ten thousand blessings besides! We know who we are, why we are here, where we are going. Life has purpose and meaning and eternal significance.

With such glorious good news, why would we keep it to ourselves? We can't! We feel compelled to tell others that they are loved by God. That there is a Savior. That there is divine help at present and hope for the future. That their lives have an eternal purpose. Thank You for the privilege of sharing the gospel.

Surely if I am filled with Your Spirit, I will be filled with Your love for a lost and dying world of sinners separated from You. Yet I confess that I have not always been attentive to telling others about You. I have missed more opportunities than I have taken. I have been shy. Timid. Fearful of getting into a conversation that would be deeper or more hostile than I could handle. Thank You for reminding me that while You don't command me to be successful in leading people to the cross, You do command me to be faithful. Thank You that as I am faithful to share the truth, the Holy Spirit works within the hearts of those to whom I speak, convicting them of sin and their need to get right with You.[3]

I pray for those who have devoted their lives to reaching others with the gospel. Evangelists. Preachers. And especially missionaries, who have left the comfort and convenience of all that is familiar in order to step out by faith to take the good news into the nations of the world. Please give them daily bread. Draw them into Your Word; then give them personal insights, understanding, and enlightenment to fortify them for the task You have assigned them. Draw them close to Your heart in prayer. Refresh their spirits with the living water so that their burdens are lifted. Fill them until they overflow with Your Spirit so that their faith becomes contagious. Let them glimpse enough eternal fruit that they would be encouraged to persevere. Open their spiritual eyes to the day when Your throne will be surrounded by people who have been purchased by Your blood from every tribe and language and people and nation.[4] People who will be there because these missionaries were faithful to proclaim the truth here. Give them strong support from sending churches. Not just financial, material support, but personal care, interest, and compassion expressed in prayers, emails, letters, and visiting teams. Protect them as they march into enemy territory. Give them victory over the Evil One. Place an angelic guard around their marriages and their children. Raise up their children to be the next generation of missionaries, preachers, and evangelists whose hearts are on fire to share the gospel because of what they have seen modeled in their own homes.

Finally, I pray that You would blow the wind of Your Spirit over their words and their work until Your kingdom comes and Your will is done on earth as it is done in Heaven.[5] We long for the day when the kingdom of this world becomes the kingdom of our Lord and of His Christ and He reigns forever and ever.[6] To this end, make us all more mission-minded.

In the strong name of the One who left the comfort of His Home in order to save us—*Jesus,*

Amen.

He who fears God fears no man.
He who kneels before God will stand
in any situation.

—Leonard Ravenhill

A Prayer to Stay Focused

TRUE, LIVING LORD,
        I acknowledge that You are Lord. Lord of the universe, Lord of this planet, Lord of this nation, Lord of this city, Lord of this community, Lord of my life . . . You are Lord of lords. I thank You and praise You, O Lord, for Your blessings and Your grace.

I humbly confess that I too often give more weight to the pressures and stresses around me than to Your sovereign plan and awesome power. I seek out worldly wisdom rather than turning to Your perfect wisdom. I boast in my own strength rather than leaning on Yours. I tend to lose my focus on You.

Lord, help me never forget that, in a world of confusion, You are the Way. In a world of political correctness, You are the Truth. In a world of death, You are eternal Life.[1]

As I refocus on You and Your Word, give me wisdom to make decisions that are right. Give me courage to stand against that which is wrong. Give me patience to navigate my relationships with grace and truth, reflecting the light of Your love in a way that brings life to all I encounter. Give me everything I need so others may see Jesus in me.

O God, I pray for these things not because I deserve them but because You have invited me to boldly ask for Your blessing in the name of Your Son, our Savior—*Jesus.*

Amen.

Personal Prayer

Like an apple tree among the trees of the
forest
is my beloved among the young men.
I delight to sit in his shade,
and his fruit is sweet to my taste.
Let him lead me to the banquet hall,
and let his banner over me be love.
—Song of Songs 2:3–4

A Prayer of Adoration for the Bridegroom

Lover of My Soul,

My heart yearns for You. Your love is more precious than any pleasures the world has to offer. Your names are like perfume to my spirit. Redeemer, Healer, Savior, Shepherd, Master, Lord, and King. Jesus. Yeshua. I long to draw near to You.[1]

I confess that I am a sinner, imperfect in body, mind, soul, and spirit. Yet You have saved me, forgiven me, redeemed me, washed me, and—wonder of wonders— You love me! You rejoice over me with singing. I am Your delight![2] And You are my delight! I delight to be in Your presence through prayer. I delight to read Your Word and hear You whisper to my heart. I delight to be identified with You regardless of what others may say or think. And then I look up and see that You have raised the banner of Your love over me because You delight for others to know that I am Yours and You are mine.[3]

In deep waters of grief and pain, You have been with me. In fiery trials of life-threatening health issues, You have been with me.[4] When I've walked through the valley of the shadow of death, You have been with me.[5] You have embraced me and carried me as a father would carry his child. You have cradled me in Your tenderness as a mother would carry her baby.[6]

When others have slandered or betrayed me, when I've been attacked or persecuted, You have strengthened my spirit.[7] While I've been in physical or emotional pain, You have placed Your deep river of peace within my soul.[8] You have given me moments of joy at times of desperation. Sheer joy that bubbles up from the wellspring of my love relationship with You, filling my heart. You have given me hope that, in spite of grief and loss, the best is yet to come.

You have given me wisdom to navigate a lifelong maze of decisions.[9] You have given me opportunities to speak up for You and stand up for You. You have opened doors that others said were closed to me.[10] And You have shut doors in order to keep me in the center of Your will. You have called me into fellowship with You,[11] then sent me out on assignment after assignment that has borne eternal fruit.[12]

You are as fair as the moon, as bright as the sun, as beautiful as all the starry host in the night sky.[13] You are mine and I am Yours. All my desire is for You.[14] I want to live in the light of Your presence. I want to draw near to

Your heart. Until I see You face to face. And that will be Heaven for me.

In the name of the Bridegroom, who is coming to receive me to Himself—*Jesus,*

Amen.

The meaning of prayer
is that we get hold of God,
not of the answer.
　　　—Oswald Chambers

A Prayer to Experience Holiness

Holy Lord, Lamb of Glory,[1] I set aside these moments to look up. I see You high and exalted, seated on the throne of my heart. I acknowledge Your authority and Your greatness. No one is greater than You are, and no one is higher than You are. In the stillness, I can hear the chorus of angelic praise: "Holy, holy, holy is the Lord Almighty."[2]

You are merciful. Yes, You are!

You are loving. Yes, You are!

You are gracious. Yes, You are!

You are kind. Yes, You are!

You are faithful. Yes, You are!

How I love You for the beauty of Your character. But I would be dishonest if I did not also acknowledge that You cannot be less than Yourself. And You are also just. You are holy. You are righteous. And a just, holy, righteous Lord demands judgment for sin. Which is the message of the Cross. If there were no accountability for sin, there would be no need for the Cross. The Cross reveals Your hatred for sin. You died so that sinners could live free from the penalty of sin. You rose from the dead so that sinners could die to the power of sin.

At the cross I see You, the holy Lamb of glory, giving Your life for little dust people, and I stand amazed in the presence of the crucified Savior. The Cross reveals not only the heinousness of my sin but also the beauty of Your infinite love as You stepped in and took Your own judgment in my place.

I confess that my focus in life and even my focus in prayer have not always been on You and You alone as the Solution to my problems and the Answer to my needs. I often have acted as though I am somebody and You are not.

I confess that often I have been so focused on "them" that I don't see myself clearly. I turn to You now and ask that You shine the light of Your truth into my heart and what I feel, into my mind and what I think, so that I see myself as You see me and truly, deeply repent of my sin.

Strip me, most holy Lord, of any pride or self-righteousness or judgmentalism. Teach me to first take the plank out of my own eye before trying to remove the splinter in someone else's eye.[3] I long for You to send revival to the hearts of Your people. Let it begin right here. Right now. With me as I confess my sin and turn away from it. I want to truly experience holiness as I reflect You from the inside out.

Please cleanse me, wash me clean, for Jesus's sake.[4] I deeply desire to be holy as You are holy.[5]

For the glory of Your great name—*Jesus,*
Amen.

With Gratitude

First, I would like to offer my deepest thanks to the Lord Jesus for opening the way into the most holy place of God's presence through His own shed blood and broken body on the cross.[1] What would I do and how would I live without access to His presence as I claim the privilege of prayer?

Second, I thank God for the problems and the pain, the hard places and the hard times, the suffering and the struggles, the agony and the adversity—because He has used them all to press me closer to Him. The hardship in my life, much more so than the ease, has taught me the depths of prayer, since it has caused me to fall on my knees in humility and look to God alone for help and for answers from His Word.

Third, I would like to thank God for my incredible publishing team at Multnomah. They have been attentive, supportive, and proactive from the inception of this book until its publication. They have embraced me and the words I have put on the page. They have even used these prayers in their own team meetings. But I am especially grateful for the provision of Laura Barker as my editor. She caught the vision for this project when the book was just a concept that God had placed on my heart. From the title and subtitle, to the arrangement of the prayers, Laura has been an incredible help. Thank you, Laura.

And last, I thank you. Like me, you have struggled in prayer but haven't given up. My sincere prayer is that God will use this book to help you overcome your struggle as He draws you nearer to His heart.

APPENDIX A

The Believer's Birthright

An Alphabetized List of Blessings

> From the fullness of his grace
> we have all received
> one blessing after another.
> —John 1:16

Many years ago, our home was robbed. The front door was broken down, and everything of value was taken—silver, jewelry, cameras, and even furniture.

That night, after I talked with law enforcement officials who assured me that the thieves would not come back, I crawled into bed—under the same covers the thieves had folded back in order to remove the pillowcases from my pillows as a means of carrying what they had stolen. I was terrified. All I could think of were the countless things that could be taken from me: my home by fire, my health through disease, my children by kid-nappers, my spouse through death, my reputation through gossip . . . I felt my body becoming cold and stiff. I knew I was going into shock.

And then God began to whisper to my heart. I had been studying Ephesians, so the first two chapters were familiar to me. The third verse of the first chapter promises that we have "every spiritual blessing in Christ."

I knew that the blessings God gives through Jesus Christ could never be taken from me. So I began to list them as they are given in Ephesians 1 and 2. There were so many that I put them to the alphabet, then went to sleep peacefully.

The next morning when I awoke, I wrote down the list of blessings that no one can ever take from me. Blessings that no thieves can steal.

I want to share with you this list of blessings, which I call "The Believer's Birthright." It is my prayer that it will help stimulate your thanksgiving and praise to the One from whom all blessings flow.

We are . . .

Accepted—as accepted by God as Jesus is.
Blessed.
Chosen to belong to God.
Delivered from sin, self, and Satan.
Enlightened to understand the things of God.
Forgiven of all sin—past, present, future.

We have . . .

Grace—great riches at Christ's expense.

Hope of Heaven.

Inheritance laid up for us in Heaven.

Justification as though we had never sinned.

Knowledge of God.

Love of God.

Mercy—receiving less than the justice we deserve.

Nearness to God.

Oneness with God.

Peace that passes all understanding.

Quickening into new life.

Redemption.

Sealing of the Holy Spirit.

Truth.

Unity with other believers in the body of Christ.

Validation as authentic children of God.

Wisdom.

X-Y-Z Exaltation to live with Him in heavenly places.

Preparing Your Heart Through Confession

A List of Sins

Summertime in the South can be hot and humid, and it's made even more miserable by little gnats called no-see-ums. They bite the fire out of their victims, but they are so tiny that they're almost invisible, making them difficult to deal with.

Sin in my life is like a no-see-um. While I can fairly easily spot sin in the life of another person, I have a hard time seeing sin in my own life until it "bites me." The bite can take the form of the Spirit's conviction or someone else's rebuke or the unpleasant consequences of making a wrong choice or giving in to a wrong attitude or habit. God has effectively used the following list, adapted from the suggestion of an old-time revivalist, to help me recognize and confess my sin. I have included the list in this appendix as a resource for you.[1]

The original author suggested praying through this list of sins three times, asking God to reveal any sin that's lurking in the deep recesses of your heart. From personal experience, I've discovered it takes courage to see yourself as He does, not as you think you are. While the revelation may be painful, confession is also a healing exercise that brings cleansing and the fullness of joy, blessing, and freedom that are found in restored fellowship with God.

INGRATITUDE

List all the favors God has bestowed on you, before and after salvation. Which ones have you forgotten to thank Him for?

LOSING LOVE FOR GOD

Consider how devastated you would be if your spouse or best friend's love for you lessened even as they increasingly loved someone or something else more. Is there evidence you are lessening in your love for Him?

NEGLECT OF BIBLE READING

Double-check to see if daily Bible reading has been pushed aside by an overly full schedule. Or as you read your Bible, are you constantly preoccupied with other things? How long has it been since reading your Bible was a delight? Do you read it so casually that you don't even remember what it said after you finish?

UNBELIEF

To refuse to believe or to expect that God will give you what He has promised is to accuse Him of lying. What promise do you think He will not give you? What prayer do you think He will not answer?

NEGLECT OF PRAYER

Prayers are not spiritual chatter, offered without fervent, focused faith. Have you substituted wishing, daydreaming, hoping, or fantasizing for real prayer?

NEGLECT OF FAMILY

Do you put yourself and your needs before theirs? What effort are you making, what habit have you established, for pursuing your family's spiritual good when it requires personal sacrifice?

LACK OF CONCERN FOR THE SALVATION OF OTHERS

Do you stand by and watch friends, neighbors, coworkers, and even family members on their way to hell, yet not care enough to warn them or pray for them or even admit that's where they will end up if they don't put their faith in Jesus? Have you become so politically correct that you don't apply the gospel to those you know and love?

LOVE OF THE WORLD AND MATERIAL THINGS

Assess what you own. Do you think your possessions are yours? That your money is yours? That you can spend it or dispose of it as you choose?

PRIDE

Have you become caught up in vanity about your appearance? Do you spend more time in getting ready for church than preparing your heart and mind to worship when you get there? Are you offended, or even slightly irritated, if others don't notice your appearance?

ENVY

Are you jealous of those who seem more fruitful or gifted or recognized than you? Do you struggle with hearing others praised?

A CRITICAL SPIRIT

God gives discernment, but do you use it to find fault with others who don't measure up to your standards?

SLANDER

Do you justify unkind words as "simply telling the truth" when your intention is to cause people to think less of a person? Whose faults, real or imagined, have you discussed behind their back? Why have you done so?

DISHONORING GOD

Do you show disrespect for God by sleeping through your prayer time or showing up late for church as though He doesn't really matter? Do you give Him the leftovers of your emotions, time, thoughts, money?

LYING

Examine your words and behavior for evidence of designed deception, anything that is contrary to the unvarnished truth. What have you said that was designed to impress someone, but it wasn't the whole truth? Or was an exaggeration of the truth?

HYPOCRISY

Are you pretending to be anything more or anything less than you truly are?

ROBBING GOD

Are you wasting your time on things that have no eternal value? What about exercising your God-given gifts and talents for a fee? What are you not doing for God that you are willing to do for others—for a price?

TEMPER

Have you lost patience with a child, coworker, friend, spouse, or staff member? What cross words have you spoken lately?

BAD TEMPER

Consider whether you have so lost control of your emotions, thoughts, and words that you've abused someone else verbally. Have you lost your temper?

God is ready and willing to forgive and cleanse us of our sin, but we must . . .

"Come now, let us reason together,"
says the LORD.
"Though your sins are like scarlet,
they shall be as white as snow;
though they are red as crimson,
they shall be like wool."
—Isaiah 1:18

If we confess our sins,
he is faithful and just
and will forgive us our sins
and purify us from all unrighteousness.
—1 John 1:9

In him [Jesus Christ]
we have redemption through his blood,
the forgiveness of sins,
in accordance with the riches of God's grace.
—Ephesians 1:7

Notes

2, "When God puts a burden," L. B. Cowman, *Streams in the Desert* (Grand Rapids, MI: Zondervan, 1965), September 30.

6, "Men ask for a rainbow," George Matheson, "Service by the Sorrowful," in *Times of Retirement: Devotional Meditations* (New York: Fleming H. Revell, 1901), 170.

10, "A true prayer is an inventory," C. H. Spurgeon, "The Power of Prayer and the Pleasure of Praise," in *The Power of Prayer in a Believer's Life,* ed. Robert Hall (Lynnwood, WA: Emerald Books, 1993), 94.

14, "The best disposition for praying," Augustine, quoted in Nick Harrison, *Magnificent Prayer: 366 Devotions to Deepen Your Prayer Experience* (Grand Rapids, MI: Zondervan, 2001), June 4.

22, "There is no way of learning faith," A. B. Simpson, *Days of Heaven upon Earth: A Year Book of Scripture Texts and Living Truths* (Nyack, NY: Christian Alliance, 1897), 218.

26, "Do not pray for easy lives," Phillips Brooks, *Christ the Life and Light: Lenten Readings,* ed. W. M. L. Jay (London: Macmillan, 1905), 209.

34, "Turn the Bible into prayer," Robert Murray McCheyne, letter, August 8, 1836, quoted in Andrew A. Bonar, *The Life and Remains, Letters, Lectures, and Poems of the Rev. Robert Murray McCheyne,* in *The Works of Robert Murray McCheyne: Complete in One Volume* (New York: Robert Carter & Brothers, 1874), 48.

42, "It is such a comfort," L. B. Cowman, *Streams in the Desert* (Grand Rapids, MI: Zondervan, 1965), July 6.

50, "The ineffable secrets are revealed," Jeanne-Marie Guyon, quoted in "Young America, No. 2: Religion and Philosophy," *The Presbyterian Quarterly Review,* no. 8 (March 1854), in *The Presbyterian Quarterly Review,* ed. Benjamin J. Wallace, vol. 2 (Philadelphia: Willis P. Hazard, 1854), 684.

54, "It is in the personal presence," Andrew Murray, *With Christ in the School of Prayer: Thoughts on Our Training for the Ministry of Intercession* (New York: Fleming H. Revell, 1885), 80–81.

78, "Prayer is the practice of drawing," Oswald Chambers, *My Utmost for His Highest,* ed. James Reimann, updated ed. (Grand Rapids, MI: Discovery House, 1992), June 26.

82, "Prayer does not fit us," Oswald Chambers, *My Utmost for His Highest,* classic ed. (Grand Rapids, MI: Discovery House, 2017), October 17.

92, "I don't believe that there is such a thing," Theodore L. Cuyler, "God's Promises," *The Christian Work and the Evangelist,* August 11, 1906, 172.

96, "All real prayer is simply asking," Samuel Cox, "The Scope of Prayer," in *Expositions* (New York: Thomas Whittaker, 1885), 243.

104, "Every life that would be strong," L. B. Cowman, *Streams in the Desert* (Grand Rapids, MI: Zondervan, 1965), December 4.

112, "The Christian on his knees," D. L. Moody, *One Thou-*

sand and One Thoughts from My Library (New York: Fleming H. Revell, 1898), 59.

116, "Prayer is an earnest," John Knox, "Treatise on Prayer," in *Select Practical Writings of John Knox* (Edinburgh, 1845), 31–32.

120, "The surrender to God," Andrew Murray, *With Christ in the School of Prayer: Thoughts on Our Training for the Ministry of Intercession* (New York: Fleming H. Revell, 1885), 157.

138, "The secret prayer chamber," O. Hallesby, *Prayer,* trans. Clarence J. Carlsen (Minneapolis: Augsburg Fortress, 1994), 99.

152, "For resurrection-stillness," Emily Steele Elliott, "Psalm 37:7," in *Chimes for Daily Service: Being Hymn-Thoughts Chiefly for the Sick or Sorrowing* (London: Haughton, 1880), 6.

156, "It is not by eloquent sermons," D. L. Moody, *Prevailing Prayer: What Hinders It?* (Chicago: F. H. Revell, 1884), 12–13.

164, "He who fears God," Leonard Ravenhill, *Why Revival Tarries* (Minneapolis: Bethany House, 2004), 24.

172, "The meaning of prayer," Oswald Chambers, *My Utmost for His Highest,* classic ed. (Grand Rapids, MI: Discovery House, 2017), February 7.

A Prayer of the Weary

1. Hebrews 4:15.
2. Isaiah 42:3.
3. Isaiah 40:28.
4. Psalm 68:6.
5. Ephesians 6:17.

A Prayer for Stormy Days

1. Job 38:4–11.
2. Mark 4:35–39.
3. Isaiah 43:2.

A Prayer in the Hardest Times

1. Habakkuk 2:1.
2. Isaac Watts, "O God, Our Help in Ages Past," 1719, public domain.
3. Psalm 23:1, 4.
4. Isaiah 53:3.
5. Hebrews 13:5.

A Prayer of Surrender

1. "Fairest Lord Jesus," verse 4 translated by Joseph A. Seiss, public domain.
2. Psalm 86:15.
3. 2 Corinthians 12:9.
4. Joel 2:12–14.
5. Psalm 18:2; 62:8.

A Prayer for Peace and Protection

1. John 3:16.

A Prayer for Unshakable Trust

1. Isaiah 40:25–26; Psalms 19:4, 6; 139:7–8.
2. Isaiah 59:1.
3. Psalm 2:2.
4. Psalm 46:2–3.
5. Psalm 46:6.
6. Psalm 37:14.

A Prayer to Be a Light in the Darkness

1. Exodus 15:11.
2. Revelation 7:9–10.
3. 2 Timothy 2:21.

A Prayer for God's Grace and Glory

1. Psalm 139:7–8.
2. Habakkuk 2:14.
3. Ephesians 6:11.
4. Revelation 22:20.

A Prayer to Trust in God's Provision

1. Matthew 6:28–30; 10:29; 14:14–21.
2. Genesis 22:14; Philippians 4:19.

A Prayer to the Eternal, Unchanging God

1. Exodus 3:14.
2. Micah 6:8.
3. Exodus 12:22–23.
4. Hebrews 7:25.
5. Psalm 91:2, 4, 11, 15.

A Prayer to the Rock of Our Salvation

1. Hebrews 1:3.
2. Psalm 2:1–2.
3. Psalm 46:2–3, 6.
4. Psalms 40:2; 95:1.
5. Matthew 24:6.

A Prayer of Worship: God's Personhood

1. Philippians 2:6–11.
2. John 14:18.
3. 1 Corinthians 13:12.
4. 1 Corinthians 10:13.
5. 1 John 3:2.

A Prayer of Worship: God's Presence

1. Genesis 1:1; John 1:1–2.
2. Genesis 2:7.
3. Exodus 7–12.
4. Exodus 14:21–22.
5. Joshua 6:1–20.
6. Daniel 3.
7. Daniel 6:13–27.
8. Ezekiel 1:1–4.
9. Isaiah 6:1.

10. Matthew 5:1–12; Luke 2:1–16, 51–52; John 19:17–18; 20:1–18; Acts 1:4–9; 2:1–4; Ephesians 1:20–23.
11. Hebrews 13:8.

A Prayer of Worship: God's Power

1. Ephesians 3:20; 2 Timothy 1:12.
2. 2 Corinthians 9:8.
3. Hebrews 2:18.
4. Hebrews 7:25.
5. 2 Timothy 1:12.
6. 2 Corinthians 3:18.
7. Jude 24.
8. Philippians 1:6.

A Prayer for the Persecuted

1. Genesis 17:1.
2. Joshua 5:14.
3. Matthew 28:18.
4. Proverbs 21:1.
5. Ephesians 6:17; Revelation 19:15.
6. Exodus 14:14.
7. Psalm 108:13.
8. 1 Corinthians 15:57.
9. Revelation 1:9–16.
10. Philippians 3:10.
11. Matthew 5:11–12.
12. Ephesians 6:11.
13. Hebrews 12:2.
14. Revelation 12:11.

A Prayer for National Cleansing and Revival

1. Isaiah 6:1.
2. Ephesians 2:4; 2 Corinthians 9:14; Exodus 34:6.
3. Isaiah 30:19.
4. Psalm 33:18.
5. Isaiah 59:1.

6. Psalm 139:7–10.
7. Daniel 9:1–19.
8. John 16:8.
9. 2 Chronicles 14:11.
10. 2 Chronicles 7:13–15.

A Prayer for the People of God

1. Portions of this prayer are adapted from *Jesus in Me: Experiencing the Holy Spirit as a Constant Companion* (Colorado Springs: Multnomah, 2019), 187–90.
2. I borrowed the analogy of our Shepherd being our spiritual GPS from Tony Evans, pastor of Oak Cliff Bible Fellowship in Dallas, Texas. See Tony Evans, *The Fire That Ignites: Living in the Power of the Holy Spirit* (Sisters, OR: Multnomah, 2003), 79.
3. Isaiah 53:6.
4. Hosea 14:1–2, 4.

A Prayer of the Lonely

1. Psalm 139:1–5.
2. Genesis 16:13.
3. Psalm 139:8–16.
4. Psalm 32:7.
5. Hebrews 13:5.
6. Matthew 28:20.
7. Revelation 22:4.
8. 1 Corinthians 13:12.
9. Revelation 21:3.

A Prayer for Victory in Battle

1. Ephesians 6:12.
2. Zechariah 4:6.
3. Revelation 19:11–14.

A Prayer for Deliverance

1. Isaiah 59:19, NKJV.
2. 2 Chronicles 20:6.

A Prayer for the Salvation of Family Members

1. Matthew 1:23.

2. John 1:14.

3. John 15:15.

4. John 1:12–13; Romans 8:15; Galatians 4:6.

A Prayer of Thanksgiving for the Power of the Cross

1. Ephesians 1:7.

2. 1 John 1:9.

3. Hebrews 10:22.

4. 1 John 5:14.

A Prayer to Make a Difference in a Hurting World

1. Isaiah 40:29; 1 Corinthians 10:13.

A Prayer of Dependence on God's Power and Authority

1. Mark 4:35–39.

2. John 2:1–10.

3. John 9:1–7.

4. Mark 5:35–42; Luke 7:11–15; John 11:38–44.

5. Proverbs 8:29.

6. Isaiah 40:26.

7. Nahum 1:3.

A Prayer of Contrition

1. Exodus 15:6–7.

2. Exodus 34:6–7.

3. Nahum 1:3.

4. Ezra 9:6, 10.

5. Daniel 9:5.

6. Romans 1:18, 23.

7. Micah 6:8.

8. Exodus 15:6; Zechariah 4:6.

A Prayer for True Wisdom

1. Romans 16:27.

2. 1 Corinthians 1:24, 30; Colossians 2:3.

3. Isaiah 55:9; Romans 11:33.
4. Proverbs 9:10.
5. Proverbs 3:5.
6. James 1:5.

A Prayer for True Security and Prosperity

1. Isaiah 40:12, 22.
2. 1 Thessalonians 5:17.
3. Joshua 23:10.
4. 2 Corinthians 12:9.
5. 1 John 4:4.

A Prayer to Live Boldly for God's Glory

1. Revelation 5:1–14.
2. Mark 10:45.
3. Proverbs 18:10.

A Prayer for Strength to Stand

1. John 1:10–11.
2. Hebrews 12:2.
3. John 1:9.
4. Acts 4:12; Philippians 2:9.
5. John 1:29.
6. Genesis 1:1; Colossians 1:16.
7. Genesis 1:11–12, 21, 24–25.
8. Genesis 1:27.
9. Genesis 2:24.
10. Genesis 1:27.
11. Psalm 139:13.
12. Psalm 2:1.
13. Psalm 40:2.

A Prayer of Confession and Repentance

1. Psalm 136:1.
2. Psalm 119:89–90.
3. 2 Peter 1:3.

4. John 1:16.
5. Joel 2:13.
6. 1 John 1:9.
7. Hebrews 4:15.
8. 2 Corinthians 5:21.

A Prayer for Restored Beauty in the Body of Christ
1. Colossians 1:18.
2. Matthew 5:14.
3. Ephesians 5:23.

A Prayer to Overcome Evil with Good
1. Psalm 19:4.
2. Psalm 147:4.
3. Proverbs 8:29.
4. Matthew 6:28–30; 10:29.
5. Psalm 139:2–4, 14, 16.
6. Revelation 5:12.
7. 2 Corinthians 11:14; 1 Peter 5:8.
8. 2 Kings 6:16–17.
9. 1 John 4:4.
10. Matthew 6:10.

A Prayer to Be Salt and Light
1. Colossians 1:16.
2. Ephesians 1:20–22.
3. Matthew 11:28; John 14:13–14.
4. Hebrews 10:19–20.
5. Hebrews 10:22.
6. John 12:32.
7. Galatians 5:22–23.
8. Philippians 3:10.
9. Matthew 5:13–14.
10. 1 John 2:28.
11. Ephesians 5:27.
12. Revelation 21:22–27.

A Prayer for an Outpouring of the Holy Spirit
1. Revelation 21:6.
2. 1 Corinthians 15:52; 1 Thessalonians 4:16–17.
3. 1 Kings 18:30–38.
4. Hebrews 13:8.

A Prayer to Live for a Greater Purpose
1. Jeremiah 9:24.

A Prayer for Future Generations
1. Psalm 90:1.
2. Psalms 100:5; 102:12; 105:8; 145:13; Ephesians 3:21.
3. Psalm 119:89.
4. Matthew 5:18.
5. 1 Corinthians 3:11.
6. Proverbs 1:7.
7. Isaiah 60:1–2.
8. Deuteronomy 28:1–6.
9. Many of these phrases come from Ephesians 1:17–18 and Colossians 1:9–12.
10. 2 Timothy 1:7–8.
11. 1 Timothy 6:10–11.
12. Romans 16:19.
13. Jude 24.

A Prayer for the Mission-Minded
1. Hosea 13:14.
2. Hebrews 2:14–15.
3. John 16:8–11.
4. Revelation 5:9.
5. Matthew 6:10.
6. Revelation 11:15.

A Prayer to Stay Focused
1. John 14:6.

A Prayer of Adoration for the Bridegroom

1. Song of Songs 1:3–4.
2. Zephaniah 3:17.
3. Song of Songs 2:4, 16.
4. Isaiah 43:2.
5. Psalm 23:4.
6. Song of Songs 2:6.
7. Ephesians 3:16.
8. Isaiah 66:12.
9. James 1:5.
10. Revelation 3:8.
11. 1 Corinthians 1:9.
12. Acts 26:15–18.
13. Song of Songs 6:10.
14. Song of Songs 7:10.

A Prayer to Experience Holiness

1. This prayer is adapted from *Jesus in Me: Experiencing the Holy Spirit as a Constant Companion* (Colorado Springs: Multnomah, 2019), 180–82.
2. Isaiah 6:3.
3. Matthew 7:1–5.
4. 1 John 1:9.
5. 1 Peter 1:15–16.

With Gratitude

1. Hebrews 10:19–22.

APPENDIX B | Preparing Your Heart Through Confession

1. Taken from *The Daniel Prayer* by Anne Graham Lotz. Copyright © 2016 by Anne Graham Lotz. Used by permission of Zondervan. Adapted specifically from *The Daniel Prayer: Prayer That Moves Heaven and Changes Nations* (Grand Rapids, MI: Zondervan, 2016), 126–28.

About the Author

Called "the best preacher in the family" by her late father, Billy Graham, Anne Graham Lotz speaks around the globe with the wisdom and authority of years spent studying God's Word.

The *New York Times* named Anne one of the five most influential evangelists of her generation. Her Just Give Me Jesus revivals have been held in more than thirty cities in twelve countries, with hundreds of thousands of attendees.

Anne is a bestselling and award-winning author of eighteen books. She is the president of AnGeL Ministries in Raleigh, North Carolina, and served as chairperson of the National Day of Prayer Task Force from 2016 to 2017.

Whether a delegate to the World Economic Forum's annual meeting, a commentator in the *Washington Post,* or a groundbreaking speaker on platforms throughout the world, Anne's aim is clear: to bring revival to the hearts of God's people. And her message is consistent: calling people into a personal relationship with God through His Word.

ANGEL MINISTRIES

5115 Hollyridge Drive

Raleigh, NC 27612-3111

(919) 787-6606

info@AnneGrahamLotz.org

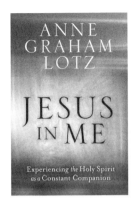

Jesus in Me

Experiencing the Holy Spirit as a constant companion

Anne Graham Lotz

We may know something about God and something about Jesus, but what do we know about the Holy Spirit? Too often we seem to overlook the third person of the Trinity, perhaps because we don't know much about Him. He seems mystical. Reserved for superspiritual Christians. We might even say He intimidates us—or somehow seems optional.

Anne Graham Lotz has good news for us. As children of God, we have the Holy Spirit in us—to counsel, to comfort, and to guide us. In Jesus in Me, Anne explores the personal and practical implications of seven aspects of the Holy Spirit in the life of a believer, including His presence, purpose, power, and provision.

She observes, "One of my deepest, richest joys has been discovering by experience who the Holy Spirit is in every step of my life's journey. Each name that He has been given—Helper, Comforter, Advocate, Intercessor, Counselor, Strengthener, and Standby—reveals another aspect of His beautiful character and has provoked in me a deep love for the One who is my constant companion…Jesus in me."

Understanding the Holy Spirit's presence in us is life-changing and world-changing. Discover how you can better love and rely on the person of the Holy Spirit—and embrace how much He loves you.

978-1-78893-111-3

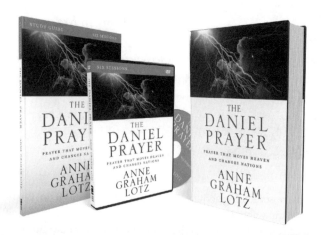

JOIN ANNE GRAHAM LOTZ AS SHE TEACHES YOU
HOW TO PRAY EFFECTIVELY FOR YOUR NATION,
FOR YOUR FAMILIES, AND FOR YOURSELF.

Many people today find that their prayers don't "work." And like a broken cell phone, DVD player, or TV remote, they throw prayer out as unnecessary "clutter" in their busy lives. Anne Graham Lotz has found that while prayer does work, sometimes the "pray-ers" don't. So she has turned to the prophet Daniel for help.

The Daniel Prayer is born deep within your soul, erupts through your heart, and pours out on your lips, words created by and infused with the Spirit of God quivering with spiritual electricity. It's really not an everyday type of prayer. It's a prayer birthed under pressure. Heartache. Grief. Desperation. It can be triggered by an answer to prayer, a promise freshly received, a miracle that lies just over the horizon.

For extended study into *The Daniel Prayer* message, Anne has also created *The Daniel Prayer* DVD study and study guide. Available now.

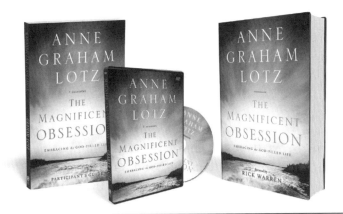

ARE YOU MISSING THE ESSENTIAL TO A JOYFUL,
PURPOSE-FILLED LIFE? HAS YOUR FAITH LOST ITS FIRE...
OR EVEN ITS MEANINGFULNESS?

Are you devoted to your church or your religion but still struggle with its practical relevance to daily life?

Are you a good person, working hard, contributing to your community, yet find life is somehow incomplete and hollow at the core?

Are you restless in your spirit, with a nagging sense that there just has to be something more?

Anne Graham Lotz has known this struggle, too. As she searched for answers to her heart's yearning and emptiness, Abraham walked out of the pages of her Bible and into her life.

Abraham's life was full of twists and turns, riches and losses, deceit and redemption, failure and success. Nevertheless, his story held the key to satisfying Anne's hungry heart. The key: embracing a God-filled life. Challenged by Abraham's example, Anne began a lifelong pursuit of knowing God. Through personal anecdotes, unforgettable stories, and inspiring insights, she shared answers found as she has embraced the God-filled life.

For extended study into the life of Abraham, Anne has also created an accompanying DVD study and study guide. Available now.

Authentic

We trust you enjoyed reading this book from Authentic. If you want to be informed of any new titles from this author and other releases you can sign up to the Authentic newsletter by scanning below:

Online:
authenticmedia.co.uk

Follow us: